Titus:

Character as the Foundation of Christian Workers

Titus:

Character as the Foundation of Christian Workers

Stephen Kaung

CHRISTIAN FELLOWSHIP PUBLISHERS, INC.
NEW YORK

ISBN: 978-1-68062-094-8

Available from the Publishers at:

11515 Allecingie Parkway
Richmond, Virginia 23235
www.c-f-p.com

Printed in the United States of America

Preface

In assessing what best constitutes the testimony of the church to the world, it can be confidently declared that there is no aspect of her testimony more important than that she manifest through her members—both individually and corporately—good Christian character. In bearing before the world the testimony of Jesus it will not be accomplished so much by her teaching than by her praiseworthy character: even the character of her Head, the Lord Jesus Christ. Whereas teaching the teaching of Christ is more important than simply knowing the teaching, the church must also shine forth the testimony of Jesus by her members faithfully expressing the new life they each and together have in Christ. For though His life and His teaching are one, what truly distinguishes the church's testimony is her life in Christ, rather than her teaching about Him. And obviously good character flows from that new life.

Hence, if the church bears before the world a full testimony concerning Christ in terms of both His life and character, that will be the greatest contribution she could make to that unbelieving world. But in order for the church to make such a contribution, she must have, particularly in her leadership, servants of God whose inner personal foundation is nothing less than the possession of a sterling Christian character.

Now throughout the history of Christianity one of God's greatest laborers in the spread of the gospel was the apostle Paul. And among his many talents was the spiritual gift of knowing people. He knew who, by the Spirit's leading, could be sent to this place or that for the purpose of setting in order the expression of the church there and of thus helping to build further the house of God. Indeed, Paul surrounded himself with numerous young people who, in possession more and more of the character of Christ as their firmly-established inner personal foundation, could be used by God for such a critical task. And one of these young people was Titus, who proved himself to be faithful and reliable again and again.

This was because he not only came to possess in increasing measure a sterling Christian character but also—with Paul's instructional guidance and the Holy Spirit's indispensable help—he was exhorted by the apostle and enabled by the Spirit to exercise in the church the four most essential elements or principles necessary for her growth and maturation; and further, he was stimulated to encourage and train others in the church to undertake the same. Those four elements are: the exercise of the following three responsibilities—(a) spiritual leadership, which is actually God's leadership as expressed through His servants, (b) spiritual discipline when necessary by those who themselves have been strictly disciplined by God, and (c) sound teaching based on God's word; as well as, fourth among these key elements, the performing of good works of every kind.

Now the four messages which together form the content of this present volume are centered upon the apostle Paul's letter to his younger co-worker Titus. They have as their initial focus an examination in some depth concerning the importance for God's servants to possess the character of Christ as their inner personal foundation for Christian service. Then, after inquiring into that vital subject there is an equally in-depth examination of each of the four essentials mentioned above. It is my fervent hope and prayer that God may raise up many in the church today who by His gifting and empowering can faithfully carry out these key elements or principles. For without the operational presence in the church of these elements, whatever may be disorderly and/or nonfunctional among her members cannot be set in order nor can the house of God be built.

One final observation perhaps needs to be made here. The spiritual deficiencies and/or needs in the church may have changed somewhat since these messages were first delivered in 1982; but it is firmly believed that the four essential elements or principles which were enunciated and examined in the concluding three messages back then are nonetheless still valid today.

May God raise up in His house many young laborers in the work of the gospel like Titus who can assist in bringing back in our day the Head of the church and King of kings—even the Lord Jesus Christ.

Contents

Publishers' Note

It should be noted that this series of messages was delivered by the author over a four-day period on 11-14 February 1982. They were spoken before an audience consisting, in particular, of leading brethren and other church workers from various local assemblies who were all gathered together in attendance at a special Christian conference, but whose location could not be determined. The text of these messages were recorded and later transcribed for possible future publication. It should be further explained that in preparing these transcribed messages for today's publication, this entire book's text has been extensively edited and that numerous additional Scripture verses—both texts and/or citations thereof—have been inserted here and there where deemed necessary or helpful to the reader.

Unless otherwise indicated,
Scripture quotations are from the
New Translation by J. N. Darby.

Chapter One

Titus—a Vessel Fit for the Master's Use

Titus 1:1-4—Paul, bondman of God, and apostle of Jesus Christ according to the faith of God's elect, and knowledge of the truth which is according to piety; in the hope of eternal life, which God, who cannot lie, promised before the ages of time, but has manifested in its own due season his word, in the proclamation with which I have been entrusted, according to the commandment of our Saviour God; to Titus, my own child according to the faith common to us; Grace and peace from God the Father, and Christ Jesus our Saviour.

Titus was a young man who was raised up by God to be a vessel fit for the Master's use, and I do believe that our Master is looking for such fit vessels today. Therefore, I would like for us to see in him—and through Paul's letter to him—what constitute the preparations for the making of a fit vessel: How does God prepare a vessel?—what does God do in such a vessel?—and what does God gain from such a vessel? So I would like to review the life of Titus with you as a way of laying a foundation before we delve more deeply into Paul's letter to Titus.

Titus's name is not mentioned in the book of Acts. This is very strange in view of the fact that by the time of Acts 15 in its account of the Jerusalem Council Titus was a trusted fellow laborer of Paul's. For, from Paul's Galatian letter we learn that he was present during this period because the first mentioning of Titus is found there in relation to that Council meeting. A quick review will be helpful here. Paul and Barnabas had gone up from Syrian Antioch to Jerusalem due to a controversy. Just prior to this some brothers had come down from Jerusalem and had begun to share with the Antiochan brethren that believing in the Lord Jesus was not enough: they had to be circumcised and they had to keep the Law of Moses: only then would their initial salvation be complete.

This caused much argument among these Gentile believers in the Antiochan church because Paul and Barnabas and others strongly believed that God never required the Gentiles to keep the Law which even the Jews had not been able to keep. And most certainly circumcision had been a sign to the Jews but not to the Gentiles. In order to resolve this situation Paul and Barnabas were sent by the church in Antioch to go up to Jerusalem because that was from where this problem had come. Their intent was to solve this problem with the apostles and the elders in Jerusalem. And in referencing this journey up to Jerusalem Paul had written in Galatians 2: "… taking also Titus with me" (v.1b). Such, then, is the first mentioning of Titus in the New Testament.

In Paul's letter to Titus he addressed him as "his son in the faith that is common to" all who believe. Evidently Titus was a native of Antioch. And probably he had come to the Lord through the ministry of the apostle Paul, which is the reason Paul could say that he was his son according to the faith that is common to all believers. Hence, here we have before us for our consideration a young man saved under the ministry of Paul, a native of Antioch, and a Gentile. In this latter regard he was not like Paul's young fellow worker Timothy who had a Gentile father and a Jewish mother, but Titus was one hundred percent Gentile.

Now when Paul went up to Jerusalem for this important matter to be settled, he took Titus with him to serve as a kind of test case. It needs to be asked: Why is it that among all the young people in Antioch Paul should take this particular young person with him? There must have been a very good reason for it. Though Timothy did not hail from Syrian Antioch but from the Galatian country of Asia Minor, I believe it can be most instructive to compare and contrast the temperaments of these two young fellow workers of Paul's. For it will help us to understand why Paul chose Titus to accompany him to Jerusalem and not others in Antioch who may have been like Timothy in temperament. For indeed, these two were quite different from each other.

In carefully reading the word of God we shall find that Timothy's temperament can be defined as follows: timid, shy, introspective, very intense, emotional, somewhat ascetic, very sensitive. Titus, on the other hand, seems to have been just the opposite in temperament: his was more even-tempered, he not having been easily stirred up nor quickly discouraged. Moreover, he had a very sober and sound mind and appeared to have had a steady kind of character in him. More than likely, therefore, it was because of this quality in Titus that largely explains why Paul chose him to accompany him and Barnabas to Jerusalem. It was not only because of Titus's temperament but perhaps even more so because of his character.

Titus was raised in the church in Antioch. In reading the book of Acts we learn that this Antiochan church was not started by an apostle. As a matter of fact, it was because of the persecution up in Jerusalem that the saints there began to spread out. And some of the saints there who were not Hebrew-speaking Jews but were Cyprians and Cyrenians found their way to Antioch and began to speak to the Greek Gentiles in that city. With the result that due to God's power that was with them many came to the Lord. That was how the church at Antioch began, and the news of this came to the attention of those in the church in Jerusalem. So the church there sent Barnabas down to Antioch, yet not in any sense of attempting to govern the church in Antioch by placing her under Jerusalem's control but in the sense of desiring to have fellowship.

So the Jerusalem church sent Barnabas to Antioch to see what the Lord had been doing there; and, being a good man, when Barnabas saw what the

Lord had been doing, he was very happy; he was not in the least jealous. He encouraged them to go on with the Lord, and as a result the Lord added many believers to the church at Antioch. However, Barnabas discovered that this work was too extensive for him to handle alone, and, remembering Saul of Tarsus, he went forth to that city and, finding Saul, took him to Antioch. For a whole year thereafter they were together with the saints there. Moreover, we learn that the disciples were first called Christians in Antioch.

Now this young man Titus was saved through the instrumentality of Paul and was raised in the church at Antioch which, having a good spiritual atmosphere, meant that he received an extremely beneficial spiritual education through Paul, Barnabas and others there. For in Acts 13 we are told that there were five prophets and teachers ministering in the Antiochan church. That, then, was the spiritual atmosphere within which this young man was brought up in the Christian life; and evidently Titus showed great progress among the brothers and sisters there, especially in the area of personal character-building.

When reading Paul's letter to Timothy, it seems to me that the emphasis there is more on gifts, how this young man's gift was being developed and encouraged. But in reading the book of Titus, it appears to me to be mainly the area of character that is being stressed. This young man had developed a good solid Christian character, and because of this,

Paul took him up to Jerusalem as a praiseworthy specimen of the saving grace of the Lord Jesus.

Now as was indicated earlier, Titus is not at all mentioned in the Acts 15 narration of what happened during the quite lengthy Jerusalem Council meeting which had been called for the express purpose of resolving the crucial doctrinal controversy that had come before it. This lack of any mention of Titus in the Acts account of the Council's proceedings is most likely because Titus had probably not uttered a single word. Yet, having been brought up to Jerusalem by Paul to serve as an exemplary test case, this fully Gentile young man would most certainly have been inclined to speak forth what was on his mind and to offer his opinion. Perhaps he might even have wanted to argue a little bit there during the proceedings; nevertheless, there is no record of Titus having participated in any way verbally.

Yes, he was present as Exhibit A, and yet he was silent. This young believer allowed his seniors to talk and argue; nonetheless, he simply sat there listening to all of them speak. Now *that,* if I may say so, is a mark of exceptional character. By the grace of God this young man had developed a good solid Christian character. Indeed, Paul could depend on Titus to display proper character because he was not intimidated by those big apostles and elders in Jerusalem, nor was he swayed by any of the arguments but stood firm and resolute as a living specimen of the pure grace of God without his having had to experience the intervention of the Mosaic Law.

Hence, I believe that this young man was chosen by God through Paul because of the quality character which had been developed in him. We do not know what happened to Titus after he returned to Antioch because nothing more is mentioned about him in the New Testament record till later in one of Paul's other epistles.

The next time Titus is mentioned is in the apostle's II Corinthians letter. Paul had eventually encountered a series of major problems with the church in Corinth, even though he had been with the saints there for a year and six months. For after he had left them, other people went there and began to cause factions or parties to arise among the believers, with some people having begun to criticize Paul and having even begun to put doubts in the minds of the Corinthian saints as to his apostleship. Paul loved the Corinthian believers very much because he had begotten them as his spiritual offspring through the gospel (cf. I Corinthians 4:15).

As a consequence, Paul felt obliged to write a very strong letter to them which is what we find in I Corinthians; and after he wrote that letter he actually began thinking of revisiting them. As a matter of fact, he was thinking of visiting them twice during his travels back and forth between Asia and Macedonia; but he was not at all sure how he would be received in Corinth. He did not want to go there again and suffer if they would not repent nor listen to him. In fact, Paul was completely in the dark as to what happened after he wrote that first extant letter of his to them or what their reaction had been; and because of this, the apostle felt led to send Titus to Corinth. To say the least, it was a very difficult situation, but Paul had faith in this young man. He sent Titus to Corinth to help solve the problems there, and so Paul arranged with Titus that on the day following the latter's visit among the believers at Corinth, the two of them would meet in nearby Troas, and he would there decide whether or not thereafter he would go straight to Corinth.

Accordingly, Paul went to Troas, but Titus was not there. Though God had opened the door of the gospel for Paul in Troas, nevertheless, Paul wrote that he "had no peace because," he added, "I did not see Titus." This apostle was so concerned about the situation in Corinth that he could not preach the gospel in Troas even though there had occurred an open door for it there; so he went on to Macedonia without going back to Corinth.

In this small incident we can notice something qualitatively commendable about Titus again. What I have in mind here is that Titus, a person who was very punctual, was one who usually kept his word: if, in this case, he had arranged with Paul to meet the apostle on the second day, then Paul would have expected him to meet him at Troas because that was how this young man usually conducted himself—indeed, that was the kind of character which was in Titus. But when Paul did not find Titus there, he suspected that some justifiable reason must have detained him at Corinth; consequently, Paul, not knowing what it was, did not have peace in his heart.

Evidently Titus had delayed his departure from Corinth because of the critical situation there. From what we subsequently learn in the account of this incident it can be assumed that probably the critical situation at Corinth had almost been resolved but not quite, and Titus had therefore delayed leaving in order that he might bring a more complete report of good news to Paul. And thank God that he in fact did meet with Paul in Macedonia; and how Paul's heart was extremely comforted.

Here was a young man who had been entrusted with a most difficult task, and yet he accomplished it so well. From this incident it can be seen that Titus must have been the kind of person who was very patient but not passive, the kind of person who was very level-headed and not easily stirred nor inclined to move ahead impulsively. If that had not been the case Titus would not have been able to deal successfully with the dire situation in Corinth because of the many difficulties which had been present there. He had carried out his task so well, in fact, that Paul decided to send Titus back to Corinth again. What praiseworthy character was to be found in that young man!

At this point in our analysis of Titus as a valued fellow worker of Paul's in the gospel, we need to recognize more fully than heretofore the relationship which existed between these two servants of the Lord. And in so doing, we shall discern a further commendable facet in the character of Titus. For these insights, however, we must consult two brief passages of Paul's in his II Corinthians letter. In the first passage the apostle referred to his younger co-worker as "my brother, Titus" (see 2:13a). Interestingly, Paul never made reference to Timothy that way. This reveals the fact that there was a difference in the relationship between Paul and Titus on the one hand and Paul and Timothy on the other. This latter relationship was a very intimate one. Timothy was Paul's spiritual son in the gospel, which thus enabled the apostle to send him to wherever Paul needed him. This extremely close relationship was evidently somewhat different from that which existed between the apostle and Titus. Though Titus was likewise a spiritual son to Paul according to the faith common to all believers, nonetheless, the apostle here called Titus "my brother."

In the second relevant passage we find the apostle describing Titus in this manner: "he is my companion and fellow labourer" (8:23a). From this description we are given to see that unlike his dealing with Timothy, which was quite intimate, Paul's way in his relationship with Titus was more businesslike in tone. We must take note of the fact that this descriptive reference to Titus is to be found within the context of Paul's wish for him to return to Corinth for the purpose of making sure that the Corinthian church would fulfill her earlier-expressed desire (8:10b, 9:5a) to provide aid for the poor, impoverished saints in Judea (cf. Romans 15:25-26). And hence, the apostle did not simply instruct Titus in the following manner: "I want you to return to Corinth and finish making arrangements for the collections of the funds for the relief of the poor in Judea." On the contrary, he actually entreated, begged and urged Titus to return and complete that particular unfinished business (8:6 NASB).

Indeed, Titus himself was most anxious and open to go back because he had such faith in the Corinthian believers. For he had much love and zeal and warmth towards these Corinthian saints in spite of what they were (8:16-17). So we can conclude from this that though Titus was quite a level-headed person, he was not cold and distant in the least. He was not the type of person who was aloof, cold, and isolated from people, and who lacked warmth towards others. Far from it!

Here, then, is another indication of what kind of character Titus possessed. For consider the following observation. Some other young men, having been successful in the kind of mission Titus had been entrusted to accomplish and being anxious, like Titus, to return to the place of their success, would most likely not have waited for their authority figure to issue further instructions but would have begun to act independently. Not so with Titus. Even though he did have such a heart of warmth to return to Corinth, he waited patiently until Paul beseeched him, even begged him to go. Why was this so in the case of Titus? It was because he never acted independently. He had already learned as a young man how to work together with others; and thus, in the present instance, Titus had waited and then had voluntarily placed himself under authority (8:17b); and because of this trait in Titus, the authority of God was manifested in and through this young man. Accordingly, this is another facet in the character we can see in Titus.

Another instance in which Titus has been mentioned is to be found in Paul's letter to Titus. And from a review of this instance we can gain yet another insight into the good Christian character of this young man.

Now probably Titus had visited Paul when for two full years he was under guarded house incarceration in Rome (Acts 28:16, 30a). But after his release from that incarceration it would appear that Titus began to travel together with Paul. They went, for instance, to the eastern Mediterranean island of Crete, where it seems that there were quite a number of believers scattered throughout that island. Paul began attempting to put the house of God in order on the island, but he did not have sufficient time because of the need to visit other places. Hence, the work was unfinished, so he left Titus in Crete with the instruction that Titus should complete the unfinished business of putting the house of God in order there and to appoint elders in every city (Titus 1:5).

The situation in Crete was most difficult because the Cretans were—by nature and by their national character—always liars, like wild beasts, and lazy gluttons. That is what their own prophet had testified (see Titus 1:12 NASB). There were many problems there because of their natural character. To be changed by the saving grace of God from such poor character to good Christian character demonstrates the power of the gospel, but such transformation takes time. Evidently the changes were occurring so slowly that Paul did not have the time to finish the work and hence he left Titus behind to complete it.

As had been the case at Corinth, so once again this young man was confronted with a most difficult task. In fact, it would appear as though, whenever and wherever Paul had a challenging mission to accomplish, he would send Titus there for its fulfillment. He had such confidence in this young man because he had recognized that God had done something extremely worthwhile in him—especially in the area of character. Yet, if God could do it in a Titus He can also perform such in others. It is only those in whom God has done the work of transforming their character who can be used by Him to help other people.

So out of the wisdom which God had given Paul, the apostle left Titus in Crete to complete the unfinished work. Once more we are given to see that this young man was commissioned by Paul to accomplish a most challenging and difficult task. And that speaks volumes as to the kind of character Titus possessed.

Now having left Titus in Crete for a time, Paul states at the end of his Titus epistle that upon the arrival there of another fellow worker named Tychicus, Titus was to hurry to Nicopolis to winter with him there (3:12). So evidently, after Paul traveled around, probably he visited Ephesus and other places, then he went to Nicopolis and decided to winter there. He gave word that as soon as Tychicus (or Artemas) would arrive in Crete, Titus should go to Nicopolis to be with him for part or all of the winter season there. That probably evinces the fact that because the work there was unfinished, Paul had to send somebody else to Crete to continue the work, since he wanted Titus to be with him in Nicopolis.

There have been different interpretations regarding this situation since we do not have specific historical records; and hence, we are left with various conjectures as to what actually happened at Nicopolis. Some commentators believe that Paul was arrested by the Imperial authorities while he was wintering at Nicopolis and was subsequently taken to Rome. Others think that he actually spent the entire winter in Nicopolis and then traveled on his own to Rome; and that while he was in Rome—which was during the violent Neronian persecution of Christians—he was arrested and taken prisoner there. But it is generally believed that most likely Titus did go to Nicopolis to be with Paul.

The last mentioning of Titus is found in the apostle's II Timothy epistle. We know that this letter was written immediately prior to the time of Paul's Roman martyrdom (4:6-8 ASV), and in chapter 4:9-12 he wrote as follows to Timothy:

> **Use diligence to come to me quickly; for Demas has forsaken me, having loved the present age, and is gone to Thessalonica; Crescens to Galatia,**

Titus to Dalmatia. Luke alone is with me. Take Mark, and bring him with thyself, for he is serviceable to me for ministry. But Tychicus I have sent to Ephesus.

These verses require some explanation in relation in particular to Titus and to a lesser extent to Timothy. It was during the initial stage of Paul's second and final stay in Rome as a captive that he wrote this second extant epistle to Timothy who at the time was in Ephesus in Asia Minor. And because the apostle knew that his departure from this life was very near at hand, he now requested Timothy to come to him quickly, since Demas had abandoned him leaving him alone except for Luke. It would appear that what the apostle wrote here concerning Demas did not apply to the others mentioned in these verses; for prior to Paul's arrival at Rome from Nicopolis he had left Crescens and Titus behind, he having sent them off, respectively, to Galatia and Dalmatia because of the spiritual needs in those places.

Now with respect to Titus, the apostle had felt led to send him to Dalmatia, which some Biblical scholars believe to have been the same general area as Illyricum; and if so, then we know from Scripture (Romans 15:19) that Paul had not only visited there on one of his previous journeys but had also preached the gospel most powerfully there. And hence, this apostle to the Gentiles would have been acquainted with the spiritual needs there.

So where was Dalmatia located in that New Testament era? It, along with Illyricum adjacent immediately to its north, constituted an extensive Roman province north of Macedonia and that extended south to north along the eastern side of the Adriatic Sea opposite to the Italian peninsula on the Sea's western side.

Let us remind ourselves that the apostle had requested Titus to come join him for the winter season at the seaport of Nicopolis, situated on Macedonia's southwestern coast, and hadsubsequently sent his young colaborer off to Dalmatia. And from this bit of information it can be assumed that there must have been news which came to Paul that there was some serious spiritual difficulty there which needed to be addressed. Not surprisingly, therefore, who better than Titus could accomplish this task?

As can be gathered from all these variously cited Scripture passages related to Titus, it can clearly be discerned that throughout the life of this faithful gospel worker God was able to use him in a very special way. Indeed, if we may put the matter in modern terms, we could justifiably describe this young man as a most useful "troubleshooter"! Wherever and whenever trouble arose among the saints of God, this faithful and reliable servant of the Lord was sent forth to resolve the troubled situation. And he seems to have been most successful in accomplishing the task in every situation. Praise God!

In the final analysis, what we can clearly see manifested in this young man is the fact that what God looks for in us who would seek to serve Him are the marks of good character. That which to God is of tremendous importance in anyone whom He can use is character. It is quite true that on the one hand vision is very important for us to possess: if we do not have spiritual vision we have no direction in our Christian life; yet not only will we not have any direction for ourselves but we cannot lead other people in a proper direction. Surely, vision is an essential which is very much needed among God's people today; but parallel to vision is good Christian character.

A person may have vision, but if a sterling Christian character is not being developed in that believer, and even though that one possesses spiritual vision, very little can be accomplished through that one. Moreover, if I may be so bold to say, not only very little will be accomplished for the Lord but also much damage shall accrue through that person. It is very true, of course, that if a person has no vision, most likely the damage will not be that extensive, yet, if that person has vision but there is not the character which accompanies the vision, then the church will truly suffer for it. In Titus, though, one particular trait which we can discern most clearly is this matter of good Christian character. Its necessity in us cannot be emphasized strongly enough.

What, basically, *is* character? One dictionary definition defines it as those attributes or features which make up and distinguish an individual. Another definition describes character as that complex of mental and ethical or moral traits marking and often distinguishing a person, group or nation. Applying this latter definition to ourselves, it is not too much to assert that we all have character not unlike the Cretans; for they possessed not only character traits individually but also nationally. There can be individual traits of character and there can be national traits as well. Furthermore, from this same applicable definition we are given to see that some character traits can be naturally good while other traits, like those of the Cretans, can be naturally bad; but regardless of their being good or bad, they all have emanated from that first man to appear in time: fallen Adam, and they all—both the bad *and* the good—need to be transformed.

Moreover, in one particular sense character is never brought to birth at a person's conception; rather, it is that which is developed later in life. By which is meant that every person is born with a life, and within that life is a nature, and if the person follows this nature and practices out in life according to that nature, it will gradually be developed into what is called character.

Before we knew the Lord we all had character—some of it good and some of it bad. We were all born with that Adamic life, and in the eyes of mankind that Adamic nature is not all bad, for Adam himself was not all that bad. Nevertheless, to be complete in this assessment we must acknowledge that Adam was not all that good, either. Thus, we have all inherited this mixed Adamic life; and so, in each one of us it began to express its true nature in many different ways: some being very sinful and downright evil, while others having appeared to be what mankind would term quite good, pleasant, and even highly beneficial. BUT, in the sight of God, all these expressions of the Adamic life—whether bad *or* good—are at their root nothing but natural character traits and are therefore of no spiritual value, and in their *un*-transformed state are useless to God in the fulfilling of His will and purpose on earth.

Oftentimes we say that a certain person seems to have a very good character because he is naturally very gentle or very considerate or very sweet—with everybody having no difficulty in loving such a person. But if we honestly and scripturally bring such an assessment before God, we must confess that that person's character in and of itself has no spiritual value to God, since that which is of the flesh remains flesh and is not of the spirit in character (cf. John 3:6). On the other hand, it is probably easier to discern this truth if a person's character is bad rather than good, since if it be good we automatically assume, incorrectly, that that good is of God.

With such an assumption as that, however, more time will most likely be required for us to be delivered from it because we do not see the need. We too often rely on the good self by transferring it to the work of God, we thinking that He will be pleased by our serving Him in that manner. But according to God's word, that is totally out of the question. For whatever emanates from the old life and Adamic nature and is developed according to the old character is that which is entirely rejected by God. Indeed, because the source is wrong He has no use for such character—whether it be good or bad in nature: it cannot serve His purpose.

But thank God, upon our believing in the Lord Jesus He puts a new life in us, and with this new life there is a new nature. Indeed, that reality is what we find being described by the apostle Peter in his second epistle:

> His divine power has given us everything we need for a godly life through our knowledge of him who called us by his own glory and goodness. Through these he has given us his very great and precious promises, so that through them you may participate in [or, partake of] the divine nature having escaped the corruption in the world caused by evil desires (1:3-4 NIV).

We are told here that by God's divine power all things which relate to life and godliness have already been given to us who have believed through our saving knowledge of Christ, who called us by His glory, goodness and virtue. We may, in fact, call all the things related to life and godliness as character; and that character is like that belonging to God himself and has already been granted to us by our having come into a saving knowledge of the Lord Jesus Christ. Furthermore, by these great and precious promises we have been made partakers of God's divine nature. In other words, when we believe in the Lord Jesus, God puts His life in us, and with this Christ-life we have a new nature—even Christ's nature; and with this nature in us all the potential is there for His character to be developed in us. Just think of this a moment— the character of Christ is within our reach because His life and nature are there resident within us!

But what is then required of us is what the apostle next declares: that we must be diligent in allowing that life in us to be developed according to Christ's nature. For take heed to what Peter has to say in the succeeding verses of this highly descriptive and detailed passage, noting carefully that what he is presenting is nothing less than the actual development of character:

> ... for this very reason also, using therewith all diligence, in your faith have also virtue, in virtue knowledge, in knowledge temperance [or, self-control], in temperance endurance, in endurance godliness, in godliness brotherly love, in brotherly love love: for these things existing and abounding in you make you to be neither idle nor unfruitful as regards the knowledge of our Lord Jesus Christ; for he with whom these things are not present is blind, short-sighted, and has forgotten the purging of his former sins. Wherefore the rather, brethren, use diligence to make your calling and election sure, for doing these things ye will never fall; for thus shall the entrance into the everlasting

kingdom of our Lord and Saviour Jesus Christ be richly furnished unto you (1:5-11).

First, God puts a new life in us and with this new life there is also a new nature—even the life and nature of Christ. All the potential is there, but we need to use diligence—"make every effort" (NIV)—to allow this life and nature to be developed and continually increased within us in the forming of Christ's character in us. Therefore, on our part we need to exercise diligence.

How is this going to be developed in us? Yes, we say we need to exercise diligence. If, however, upon our believing in the Lord Jesus we are careless and not diligent, if we do not pay attention to the new life and nature within us, if we still walk according to the flesh, if we still permit old habits to remain in us—if, in short, we do not use diligence to cultivate the new character of Christ, then we are still living and walking according to the flesh and not according to the Spirit (cf. Romans 8:4b), and thus there is no transformation taking place in us. So on our part there needs to be diligence.

However, it needs to be inquired: In what form or in what manner is this diligence of ours to be implemented and manifested? Is it not for us to make every effort to continually allow the Holy Spirit to perform His transforming work in us? Indeed, the work of God's Spirit is essentially that of developing the Christ-character in us. Let us thank God that He has given us the Holy Spirit who dwells in every believer. It is by the Holy Spirit that our Father-God himself takes up His abode in us. Why does He do this? Why does He make His permanent home in us? For we are informed in Scripture that in making His home in us by the Holy Spirit, He will never leave us nor forsake us (Hebrews 13:5b quoting God's own words to Joshua found in Joshua 1:5). Surely this is something most precious, and for which we can thank God; because although we may grieve the Holy Spirit and we may even quench His holy influence upon our lives, we will never be able to drive Him away: in fact, the Holy Spirit comes to stay.

Let us realize afresh that on the day that you believed in the Lord Jesus the Holy Spirit not only quickened and made alive your heretofore dead spirit and made it new, He also came and now dwells in your new spirit. The Holy Spirit and your new spirit have borne witness together that you are a child of God (Romans 8:16), and of this they continue to assure you. And now the chief work or task of the indwelling Holy Spirit is to develop the Christ-character in you and me.

Perhaps it will be helpful here to quote two passages of Scripture related to the Holy Spirit's main task in the believer. One is from the apostle Paul which at first references the ministry of the Law and of the letter at the time of Moses and the Israelites but then, in contrasting language, proceeds to describe the ministry of the Spirit for God's people today. And the other passage is from the apostle John who details what the Lord Jesus himself had to say to His disciples about that same primary task of the Holy Spirit.

> ... if the Law [or, if the ministry of the letter] which fades away came with glory, how much more must ... [the ministry of the Spirit] which remains and is permanent abide in glory and splendor! Since [, then,] we have such a glorious hope and confident expectation, we speak with ... great ... [boldness], and we are not like Moses, who used to put a veil over his face so that the Israelites would not gaze at the end of the glory which was fading away. But in fact their minds were hardened for they had lost the ability to understand; for until this very day at the reading of the old covenant the same veil remains unlifted, because it is removed only in Christ. But to this day whenever Moses is read, a veil of blindness lies over their heart; but whenever a person's heart turns to the Lord, the veil is taken away. Now the Lord is the Spirit, and where the Spirit of the Lord is there is liberty ... [for men's souls to be set free— Phillips]. And we all, with unveiled face, continually seeing [reflected] as in a mirror the glory of the Lord, are progressively being transformed into His image from one degree of glory to even more glory, which comes [just as would be expected—DLNT] from the Lord who is the Spirit (II Corinthians 3:11-18 Amplified).

… the Advocate, the Holy Spirit, whom the Father will send in my name, will teach you all things and will remind you of everything I have said to you. … When the [Holy Spirit as] Advocate comes, whom I will send to you from the Father— the Spirit of truth … —he will testify about me. … He will glorify me because it is from me that he will receive what he will make known to you. All that belongs to the Father is mine. That is why I said the Spirit will receive from me what He will make known to you (John 14:26, 15:26, 16:14-15 NIV).

From these passages it becomes clear that the Holy Spirit's primary task in us believers is to show or make known Christ to us in an ever-increasing manner so that in seeing Him with an unveiled face our character shall gradually be transformed into the character of Christ himself, it occurring from one degree of glory to another according to His very own image.

However, as Paul's passage makes clear, this can only take place as we turn our hearts towards the Lord. But that is where the believer's diligence comes into play in this matter. We must make every effort to turn our hearts continually to the Lord Jesus and behold His beauty, His glory, His splendor; and as we do so, the Holy Spirit will perform His transforming work in developing the Christ-character in us until His very character distinguishes us.

If this be true, as it most surely is, and if we wish to be used by God in whatever capacity it may turn out to be, then we will have to apply ourselves in the most diligent manner. Let us continually allow the Holy Spirit to make known to us all which He desires to show us about Christ; and by such diligent turning of our hearts to the Lord, we shall behold Him with unveiled face to such an extent that we shall begin to reflect, as in a mirror, the glory of the Lord Jesus himself. And thus do we grant to the Holy Spirit the liberty to transform our fallen character into the glorious character of Christ.

From these various observations it becomes obvious that the reason we may not be experiencing the work of the Holy Spirit in transforming our character into that of Christ is because we do not allow the Spirit to show more of Christ to us; and hence, since we see less and less of Christ, we willy-nilly focus our sight upon ourselves more and more; with the result that we continue to work out our Christian life according to the fallen character of the old Adamic life.

The solution to our problem is for us not only to turn our hearts to the Lord but also to be diligent in keeping our hearts turned towards Him. Only as we do that can the Holy Spirit bring His transforming work in us to completion. Do let us therefore realize this, that to the extent in which the Christ-character is being developed and increased in us will be the extent to which God can effectively use us in His service.

Now in returning to our discussion of the young man Titus we clearly see that the character of Christ was continually being developed in him, it resulting in his being used by God as a most effective troubleshooter again and again in helping many of God's people—especially those believers in difficult situations. Indeed, because of the transforming work of the Holy Spirit in him, Titus was able to inspire such needy believers to turn to the Lord and, in seeing Him afresh, their dire difficulties and problems were resolved to God's satisfaction.

Let us see that in any discussion on Christian leadership training, discovering various methods and techniques can certainly be of help—and we should learn about them. Nevertheless, as can be seen in the experience of Titus, the most essential ingredient in leadership is the element of character development. In fact, without this having been accomplished by the Holy Spirit in this young man, the apostle Paul could never have written Titus 1:5:

The reason I left you in Crete was that you might straighten out [and put in order] what was left unfinished [by me] and appoint elders in every town, as I directed you (NIV).

The commission which Titus received from Paul was to set the house of God in order. Let us recognize that God really has but one work to do. It is quite true that in one sense He has many works to be accomplished; but in another sense those many works are meant to contribute to the accomplishing of the one overarching work just mentioned. As the Lord Jesus once observed: "My Father is working until now, and I Myself am working" (John 5:17 NIV). And on another occasion He declared to His disciples that believers in Him would do the works which He himself was doing (cf. John 14:12a).

Now we are told in the book of Hebrews that back in the time of Abraham, the founding patriarch of the Israelites, he had looked forward by faith to the city with foundations whose Architect and Builder is God himself (11:10 NASB). And so God proceeded to work among the Israelites to build them into a peculiar—that is, a special—people unto the Lord. And that was the work of God back then.

Much later, in the time of the New Testament era and beyond—that is to say, even also in our own time today—God is gathering together unto the name of the Lord one people from all tribes, tongues, peoples, and nations (Revelation 5:9, 7:9) in order that they may be constituted as the house of God. God's one work in our time can therefore be described as the building up of the house of God which is the church.

And we are further told in Scripture (in Revelation 21:2, 10 ff.) that eventually—at the very end of time—we shall behold New Jerusalem: she representing the consummation of all God's working from the very beginning to the very end. Indeed, New Jerusalem is (a) that city with foundations which Abraham had looked forward to, (b) that commonwealth of Israel which God had worked to create, and (c) that building up throughout these last two millennia of the church of God—all such being facets of the one work of God. For let us further be reminded from the book of

Revelation (21:12-14) that the names to be inscribed on the twelve gates of New Jerusalem shall be those of the twelve tribes of Israel, and that the names to be inscribed on New Jerusalem's twelve foundations shall be those of the twelve apostles of the Lamb, even the Lord Jesus Christ.

We can discern from all the above data, therefore, that all the works of God are to be consummated into the one new reality: New Jerusalem. That is, and always has been, God's work from time's very beginning; and it has been but one single work. It is quite true, of course, that His work may have appeared differently throughout the different ages of time: yet it has all been one work. And the manifestation of that one work throughout New Testament times and during our own period today has been, and still continues to be, the building of the church, the house of God.

God's one work today includes, of course, several important activities—the preaching of the gospel, personal and group evangelism, the drawing of people into the house, etc., etc.—so that there will be material for the building of God's house. For after believers in Christ are brought in, they need to be built together into the dwelling place of God. Bringing believers in and treating them, as it were, as simply a piled-up heap of stones is not a sufficient work to satisfy the heart of God. On the contrary, His house is an organic structure; and hence, all material being brought in must be set in order if God's house is to be built up to His satisfaction.

Now with respect to the situation on the isle of Crete, evidently it was not just in one town or city that many believers had been brought into the church but in many Cretan communities this had occurred. And so, the great task required to be done there was to build the house of God and set all things in order in the various local churches which had been established. And the commission of Paul to Titus was to accomplish that very task of straightening out what had descended into disorder among this island's believers.

We can therefore deduce from this situation that setting the house of God in order cannot be accomplished by any technical or mechanical means or methods. Had that been all which would have been required, the apostle would have completed the task himself in a few short days. He could have gathered together all the saints in all the various communities, appointed a few elders and deacons in each place, have then set everything in order, and, having completed the work, he could have departed. Clearly, though, Paul was not able to do so during the brief time he was there.

Allow me to speak most plainly here. To set in order the house of God which may be in disorder and even in chaos, one must undertake the task according to spiritual life; and thus, it being a matter of spiritual life, such a task requires, first of all, the possession of Christ's character on the part of God's worker. And then, the worker's task is to build with character by instilling that same character in the believers—especially in those who shall emerge as leaders. It becomes obvious, therefore, that such a work cannot be rushed.

Setting the house of God in order cannot be achieved if God's servant enters into a disorderly church situation with the notion of simply gathering the saints together and, by appointment, filling church offices, and then, confidently declaring: "That's it! God's house here is now in order, and I can now depart." Such an outward mechanical solution as that will not work. Even the apostle Paul could not, and did not, follow that course of action. Instead, he realized that the fulfillment of the task must be carried out according to life; which meant that a much longer period was necessary if the work was to be completed—and completed well. That is why Paul, who could not remain longer in Crete, had to leave Titus behind to finish the unfinished work.

What was therefore required if God's disorderly house in Crete was to be set in order was for God's worker—Titus—to be in possession of the character of Christ, which he did indeed possess, and then to develop that same character in the saints there. And thus we see that what was needed first and foremost in these Cretan believers was not the outward application of some mechanical method or technique—such as the appointment of church officers—but was the development and growth of spiritual life, which involves the building up of character. The setting in order of God's house is brought about from within out of the inner life with the Lord and not, in the first instance, by initiating some action from outside.

We who are God's people need to recognize that the commission which Titus had received is the same commission which is to be ours. Whether we are engaged in God's work as a worker or as a leading brother or sister, we are all engaged in this vital task of setting God's house in order so that He may dwell in His house in peace and may feel comfortable to rest in it.

Titus, of course, was a young worker who had been commissioned to set the house of God in order in Crete. And we, too, have been commissioned to engage in the same work in one way or another in different capacities. That is why I believe this letter of Paul's to Titus is very important for us to grasp hold of, seeing as how the many instructions which the apostle had given throughout his epistle to this young worker can serve as those ways by which we in our day can be used by God to set His house in order.

God willing, therefore, I would like for us to consider together four key areas of instruction covered by this letter to Titus which I sincerely believe must be present in, and applied practically to, God's house in our day if we are to fulfill our own commission before the Lord of setting in order today's expression of the house of God. Those key areas of instruction have to do with the following topics: one, good and effective leadership; two, discipline; three, sound teaching; and four, good works. These four areas of instruction were emphasized and reemphasized in this epistle; and it was the lack of these four which had caused all the disorder and chaos in the churches in Crete.

As we move forward as God's workers, may the Lord by His Spirit help us to see clearly the importance of these areas of instruction to be found in God's word; and that in seeing their importance, and in implementing them practically, we may be helped in fulfilling our own commission before the Lord.

Our heavenly Father, in laying these important matters before the brethren here, we are compelled to inquire of Thee, Who is competent to undertake such things? We can only acknowledge that whatever competence we have is of Thee alone. If it is Thy will that we should be involved in the building of Thy house, and if, further, it is Thy will that Thy house should be set in order, and we know that it is, then we look to Thee for Thy grace, Thy mercy, and Thy working in us so that we may be able to be used of Thee to help our brothers and sisters in such a way that Thy church may truly be Thy home and a place of rest for thyself. Oh God, this is our desire, and we just look to Thee to help us as we go forward in Thy service. We ask in the name of our Lord Jesus. Amen.

Chapter Two

Setting God's House in Order: Leadership

Titus 1:5-14—For this cause I left thee in Crete, that thou mightiest go on to set right what remained unordered, and establish elders in each city, as I had ordered thee: if any one be free from all charge against him, husband of one wife, having believing children not accused of excess or unruly. For the overseer must be free from all charge against him as God's steward; not headstrong, not passionate, not disorderly through wine, not a striker, not seeking gain by base means; but hospitable, a lover of goodness, discreet, just, pious temperate, clinging to the faithful word according to the doctrine taught, that he may be able both to encourage with sound teaching and refute gainsayers. For there are many and disorderly vain speakers and deceivers of people's minds, specially those of the circumcision, who must have their mouths stopped, who subvert whole houses, teaching things which ought not to be taught for the sake of base gain. One of themselves, a prophet of their own, has said, Cretans are always liars, evil wild beasts, lazy gluttons. This testimony is true; for which cause rebuke them severely, that they may be sound in the faith, not turning their minds to Jewish fables and commandments of men turning away from the truth.

It was mentioned last time that Titus was a young man raised up by God to become a useful vessel in His hand. Most probably he was a native of Antioch itself. He came to the Lord through the instrumentality of the apostle Paul and received his spiritual education in the Antiochan church. As was indicated previously, it would appear that not only Titus but also young Timothy were both raised up by God and trained in the local assemblies where they were at the beginning stage of their spiritual lives. And I would heartily agree that according to one's understanding of the New Testament the local assembly where a believer may be situated is the best training ground for him or her. God is not as much interested in mass production as He is in raising people up one by one. And He does this in the most practical environment there is—which is to say that in whatever local assembly of the saints He places you is the place where your training to be His fit vessel should begin.

Many saints look elsewhere to be trained, they ignoring or forgetting that the place where God has put them is their best training ground; consequently, how often they miss out on the kind of training which God desires to give them. We should therefore avail ourselves of God's desired training in the place locally where we are situated.

Evidently it was in Antioch's local assembly where Titus had been trained and where his Christian character had been developed, built up, and proven. In fact, he had apparently made such excellent progress that it soon manifested itself, and to such an extent that Paul had felt it safe to take Titus with him to Jerusalem where he could serve as Exhibit A in reflecting the power of Christ in transforming a full-fledged Gentile and unbeliever into a Christian possessed of a solid foundation in character. This young man was a very good specimen, indeed, without there having been the intervention or interference of the Mosaic Law in his conversion and subsequent development as a Christian.

From that time onward Titus began to be used by God in working together with the apostle Paul. As a consequence, he was sent by the apostle to various local churches for the purpose of resolving their difficult situations. Titus performed this task as though he were a spiritual public troubleshooter, and God used him greatly in this way.

Now in analyzing the life of Titus I believe we shall discover that the secret of his usefulness to God was none other than that he possessed a sterling Christian character which was well-rounded in every way: diligent, faithful, punctual, and not afraid to work. Some believers are afraid of giving themselves to working, but here was a young servant of God who was not afraid to confront the most difficult church situations imaginable. Moreover, he was level-headed but not coldly rational, patient, and also firm in his resolve to work diligently in solving the most challenging problems. And with such a commendable character as this, Titus was able to be highly used by God.

It is my hope and prayer, therefore, that we all may deem this matter of Christian character as being most essential for anyone to have who seeks to know how best to serve the Lord.

After Paul was released from his first Roman captivity he began to travel and visit different places, he being accompanied by Titus. One such place was Crete, where there were quite a number of believers on this island who were scattered in various towns and cities. Paul began to work in their midst in an attempt to build them up together in the Lord, but he was not able to finish the work. Therefore, he left Titus behind; and this circumstance served as the motivation for Paul to pen his letter of instructions to Titus on how to continue, and hopefully finish, the needful upbuilding work begun by the apostle.

It was mentioned last time that God has only one work to do, and He has been doing this one work from the very beginning of the history of mankind and will continue doing so to the very end, which will be consummated in New Jerusalem. Moreover, in our own day this one work of God is being centered upon the building up of the church, which is the house of God. And being a most practical God, He is accomplishing this one work of His, He mainly doing so in the various local assemblies around the world.

It is true that one day we shall see the church universal truly manifested, but today, God's work in the building of the house of God is actually centered upon the building up of every local assembly. That is why in reading the book of Acts we find that in the building of the house of God He began with the church in Jerusalem and then worked with the churches in other areas and/or localities such as Judea, Samaria, Antioch, Galatia, Philippi, and Rome. And by building up these local assemblies God was building, and is continuing to build, the church universal—His completed house.

Furthermore, in chapters 2 and 3 of God's concluding book of Holy Writ—Revelation—we see the same one work of his continuing to occur. For there were seven specific local churches located in Asia Minor that were singled out by name in these two chapters. Further, we are told there that One like the Son of man was described as walking in the midst of these seven local assemblies or local churches, referred to there as seven golden lampstands. What was He doing? He was examining the saints in each assembly, and exhorting them, warning them, and helping them—He thus attempting to restore them to their former spiritual state by calling them to repent. The Son of man—even the resurrected-ascended-glorified Christ—was doing all He could with these seven local churches, with each one being directly responsible to react and respond accordingly to Him who is the Head of the church.

By the time a reader reaches the end of Revelation, those seven lampstands are no longer to be seen or mentioned. Instead, there is now but one giant lampstand being described, which is none other than New Jerusalem, because the Holy City—New Jerusalem—is seen and described as one giant lampstand (Revelation 21:23-24), with the twelve foundations mentioned there serving as the base of the lampstand. The city is this one gigantic lampstand, with the Lamb serving as its lamp and its light being the glory of God. Hence, in considering the book of Revelation as a whole, we can conclude that all the practical works of God in building His house are being accomplished in the church local wherever she is to be found on earth, as reflected illustratively in what the Son of man was doing among the seven local assemblies in Asia Minor. And when that work is completely finished, then, finally, it can be said that the church universal, which God in His one work has been building towards by means of His many practical works accomplished in the church local, will have been fully realized: even the Holy City with foundations, New Jerusalem.

Back in the time of Paul, therefore, the same practical works were being undertaken in Crete by this apostle and subsequently thereafter by Titus. For Paul had left this young man there for the purpose of continuing the work of building up the various local churches situated throughout this island. We may therefore justifiably assert that Titus was actually engaged in building the church universal by his performing all the necessary practical works at the local level. Titus was being used by God in contributing to the building up of that city with foundations which Abraham of old, and the many other devoted people of God who came after him, had by faith looked forward to seeing.

Throughout the ages past and during this present Age of Grace, wherever people have been and are yet being saved, God has been engaged in gathering to himself a people out of every tribe, tongue, people, and nation. Indeed, that is the very meaning of the Greek term *ecclesia* for our English word church: "the called out ones" from the unbelieving world. However, it has never been God's will that people be merely saved and remain as individual believers. It is quite true, of course, that a person must be individually, personally redeemed; no one can be saved on behalf of another person: a husband cannot be saved for his wife, a wife for her husband, parents for their children, nor children for their parents. Yes, people in these relationships can be helped along towards their individual salvation, but no one can serve as a substitute.

Nevertheless, after we are saved it is not God's will that we remain as individual believers because the life which we each receive at conversion is, by its very nature, "a together-life." We each share the same life of the Lord Jesus and we are thus all to be gathered together as His body, the church, with the Lord as her

Head. Accordingly, whenever people are saved, they are not to live the Christian life as isolated individuals but are to be built up together as the church, the house of God. And from the Scriptures we are given to know what we believers should do by our carefully observing how the earliest followers of Christ conducted themselves together at the very beginning of the church's existence.

From the New Testament book of Acts chapter 2 we learn that in Jerusalem on the Jewish festival day of Pentecost there were 120 of Jesus' earliest disciples who were gathered together in one place preparing themselves by earnestly praying and waiting for the Holy Spirit to descend upon them—they awaiting the "power from on high," as the resurrected Lord Jesus had instructed them to do (Luke 24:49b). And in fact, the Holy Spirit did come upon these 120: it constituting the mystery but also the real meaning of that Pentecost day.

Too often we are tremendously affected only by the sound and sight of what occurred that day—the hard-breathing sound emanating from heaven and the awesome sight of tongues as of fire alighting upon the head of each gathered believer. We must certainly thank God that such phenomena did occur that day; but the real significance of Pentecost is to be understood and appreciated as actually lying far deeper than in the outward sound and sight of that day's astonishing event; for what happened was that these 120 individual believers were all baptized together by one Spirit into the one body of Christ, as the apostle Paul would inform us later in his I Corinthians letter (12:13a NASB). That reality is the true marvel of Pentecost: that 120 individuals now become, spiritually speaking, just one body consisting of its 120 members.

Here—if we are spiritually alert—we can discern a huge difference: that a *congregation* of 120 members become a *body* of 120 members. Such a difference is as vast as heaven's distance is from earth! Think of it, that by one Spirit these all were baptized into the one single body of Christ. Then later that same day God by His grace added 3,000 more saved individuals to that one body!

Now having been brought into one, what did these believers commence doing? We are told further in Acts 2 that those who had believed "persevered in the teaching and fellowship of the apostles, in the breaking of bread and prayers" (v.42). In other words, those who were together continued constantly in the teaching and in the fellowship of the apostles. We know that the teaching of the apostles which they adhered to was none other than the teaching of Christ because the apostles took what they had received from Christ himself and then communicated it to the saints of that day. We also know that the fellowship of the apostles which those early believers experienced and enjoyed was none other than the fellowship with the Father and the Son because one of those very apostles, John himself, would long afterwards explain in his first epistle what the definition of that fellowship was, for he wrote that what "we have seen and heard we report to you [so] that ye may have fellowship with us; and our fellowship is indeed with the Father, and with his Son Jesus Christ" (I John 1:3). Hence, the fellowship of the apostles was the fellowship with both the Father and the Son by the Spirit.

Now this teaching and fellowship of the apostles was expressed back then in basically two ways: the breaking of bread and prayer. So those earliest disciples of Christ came together and broke the communion bread every day. In addition, we have seen how at the very beginning of the book of Acts that they came together to pray. Whenever these disciples had a problem they came together and prayed. They were a praying people, and in this way they were gradually growing in faith and developing in Christian character.

Moreover, in the church's beginning these believers did not have any rules or regulations given to them as to how and when to meet. Instead, they often came together, they doing so much more often than we do today. Unlike back then, modern life today is not very conducive to spiritual growth, but in those early days they met every day and labored together in prayer as well as exhorted one another.

Strangely enough, however, except in the case of the description we have in verses 26-33 of I Corinthians 14 of a special kind of meeting which the early church believers experienced when gathered together and which provides us with only a hint of how they would sometimes meet, these earliest members of the body of Christ simply met for prayer, for the breaking of bread, and perhaps for a few other purposes—yet without there having been issued any rule, regulation, or program. It was simply the factual reality that they allowed the Holy Spirit to lead them while they were together. Consequently, the saints in this early period of the church's history were quite free to grow in the Lord in the most uninhibited way.

And as they began to grow not only in number but in life, a divine order began to emerge in their midst. At first there was neither rule nor regulation, with the Holy Spirit being in full charge. But when their new life in Christ began to grow and develop, a divine order commenced evolving out of that organic body. At the very beginning of their existence as members of the body of Christ it was not something imposed upon them from outside nor organized nor controlled by the laying down of rules and regulations. On the contrary, at the outset it was simply the experiencing of the Christ-life together, and then the life grew.

However, as that life of theirs in Christ together further developed to a certain degree, a certain order began to appear involving, at first, the appointment of brethren to serve tables. It is most interesting to note that at the beginning of God's people coming together we do not see elders making their appearance. In the church at Jerusalem those whom we would today call deacons seemed to have come first, and their appearing first was because there was a need (Acts 6:1-6). Although those seven brothers chosen for this work were not called deacons at that time, we know that they were doing the work of deacons. And as for elders, it was not until later that they were present in the Jerusalem church (e.g., they are for the very first time mentioned as being present and active there, but only by the time of Acts chapter 11, verse 30.)

In this very regard, let us review how the apostles Barnabas and Saul (later called Paul) had handled this matter concerning elders. These two had been sent forth from the church in Syrian Antioch to do the work to which the Holy Spirit had called them among the Gentiles. So they traveled from city to city and people got saved and began to meet together. At this early stage these two apostles did not, at their departure from these believers, leave behind them many rules and regulations on how to meet, what to do and what not to do, and who could do what; rather, these believers were simply left in the care of the Holy Spirit for Him to develop them and let their life grow. When, though, after life had grown somewhat, Paul and Barnabas came back into their midst; and, seeing that a semblance of divine order had begun to be manifested among the saints, they commenced recognizing some as leaders and elders (Acts 14:21-23). Yes, indeed, there must be order in the local church, but it is in this or in some such similar manner and by this means that the entire element of order comes into existence in God's house—yet not merely with respect to elders but with respect to other leaders in the church as well.

That is why Paul left Titus in Crete to set the house of God in order there. There were certainly believers and there were certainly meetings, and thus they were together, but somehow there was no order. In fact, everything was in such disorder that the apostle Paul felt the time had come that the house of God locally in Crete must be set in order.

Sometimes we exhibit fear upon hearing the word order. Perhaps this is a reaction to what we have experienced in the past. We may have been on the receiving end of illegitimate human order over a lengthy period of time, including perhaps in our experience of Christianity; so that upon the mere mention of the word order we instinctively rebel against it. Furthermore, with regard to the church, we may end up going to the opposite extreme of adopting the attitude that for God's house to be truly spiritual is for it to be without order: the more disorder therein the more spiritual it will be. We may have gone so far to this other extreme, in fact, that whatever speaks of order is considered dead and not living and therefore unspiritual. Such can be, and often is, our reaction to inappropriate and wrongfully imposed human order in God's house.

It is true, of course, that if order is imposed upon the church from outside, if it be order which is organized by the hand of man, if there be rules and regulations which are legalistic and formal in character, and which bind people to the point of spiritual death—all such is definitely wrong. But to believe that for the church to be spiritual there cannot be order is equally wrong. As a matter of fact, a lack of order—which is to say, disorder—is a sign of the flesh, whereas it is intimated in Scripture that our God is a God of order and not disorder (I Corinthians 14:33, cf. v. 40).

The difference to be noted here is that divine order is the result of the growth of the life of Christ being manifested in the body of Christ, for there is an inherent order in that life; but should that order not be properly understood, recognized, and then followed, the further growth of life will be hindered. On the other hand, should that divine order be recognized and properly implemented, the entire local church as an expression of the body of Christ shall grow normally and more quickly. A stage will therefore arrive in the life experience of a local church wherein things must be set in order. Otherwise, there can be no building up of the house of God.

When building a house or some other structure, there is bound to be order involved. Placing a brick here or a piece of wood there in a random, haphazard manner does not a building make. To create any usable structure requires the element of order; otherwise, the result can only be disorder and failure in the undertaking. Moreover, the various works involved in constructing any edifice cannot be rushed if the outcome is to be a success.

Now these same requirements—order and sufficient time—are likewise necessary in building the house of God. Because all facets of our church experience together—such things as our relationship with Christ the Head and with one another, our place in God's house, our responsibility, the way we should function, how our gifts should be exercised, the matter of leadership—are all based on life, the work required in building God's house cannot be rushed. And hence, the best way to put things in order is to assist in developing the spiritual life in the brothers and sisters; and as this is being achieved step by step, divine order becomes possible and progressively makes its appearance.

Much time may therefore be necessary to be able to witness the completion of all aspects of the divine order, especially if there is a great amount of disorder and even chaos present in the church. Indeed, that was why Paul, who needed to visit other places, lacked sufficient time to finish the work himself of putting in order the highly disorderly situation in God's house in Crete. And so he felt it necessary to leave Titus behind for completing the work. However, because later the apostle wished to have Titus with him at Nicopolis during the oncoming winter season, we learn at the end of his letter to Titus (3:12) that Paul needed to send to the island another gospel worker—Tychicus—to continue the work to completion, since even by that much later time the work of putting God's house in order there was still not finished, thus further indicating how badly serious the state of the church was on the island.

I do hope that none of us will swing to the extreme of thinking that for God's house to be in order is not spiritual or is less spiritual, but rather that we will see what divine order really is, that life has to be ordered for it to fulfill its full growth.

Now it was briefly pointed out during our last time together that for God's house to be set in divine order there are four elements which in the apostle's letter to Titus were emphasized as being essential in achieving such a work. Some Christians today think that the church is a democracy—a congregational free-for-all. That again probably represents a latter-day instinctive reaction stemming from the fact that, having experienced traditional Christianity for some time but from which they may have recently come out, those Christians had discerned that the "church" they had belonged to had been so ordered and controlled by its human organization that there was no freedom whatsoever. All was programmed to such an extent that all aspects of church expression were in the hands perhaps of the pastor and that what was expected of them was simply to lay back and participate in being a good supporting audience. And hence, it is not surprising that having exited from that kind of bondage, they would go to the opposite extreme of thinking that in their new church experience it is a free-for-all environment wherein everyone can do whatever he or she wishes.

If, for instance, a church member would very much like to have a favorite hymn sung at every meeting by all present, then that one has the right to ask the brethren to sing it and has the expectation that the hymn will be sung. Or if someone has a favorite topic with which to weary the ears of all the other members present, why, that one has the right to do so. If that be the case, then the church will have become a democratically-inspired kind of do-whatever-you-want environment, there being no order, no leadership, no semblance of any spiritual authority—and therefore no evidence of submission where such be necessary according to Scripture (cf., e.g., I Corinthians 16:15-16). In short, permit me to paraphrase and apply an old familiar American saying to such a situation just now described: "Everyone is a chief, there being no one willing to be an Indian"! Is this a correct conception of what the true church, even God's house, is or should be, according to the Scriptures? Hardly!

Recently I heard a brother observe the following, he referencing a newly-established local assembly of the saints: "Now, we are a free church." By that he meant that his "church" was not controlled, directed or ruled by a pastor or by deacons, with everyone having the right to say or do or expect whatever he or she wishes; the sentiment being: "Thank God, we are now a free church!" Let me frankly declare in response that there is no such thing as a free church.

In the house of God there is to be order, so the first thing which Paul wanted Titus to set right was in regard to appointing elders. Now in our reading of Paul's letters, whether to Timothy or to Titus, it is clear that this apostle's emphasis is actually not upon the *office* of the elders but upon their *function*. And is not their function that of exercising leadership in the church? Now if that be true, then I believe we can justifiably substitute the broader-in-scope word leaders for that of elders, since elders are undeniably church leaders. Moreover, there are to be other leaders in the local church who are neither elders nor even deacons.

As an example of this from Scripture I would cite what is revealed to us in Acts chapter 15. We are told there that after the Jerusalem conference had settled—through the gathered apostles and elders there as guided by the Holy Spirit—the controversy concerning the critical doctrinal question of Law versus Grace with respect to the salvation of Gentile believers in Christ, those two sets of leaders had composed a letter outlining their decision and which was addressed to, and for the spiritual benefit of, the churches in the Gentile world. This letter was then to be carried to, and read out by, Paul and Barnabas and who were accompanied by two Jerusalem church leaders who would bear witness to the truth of that letter's contents.

Who were those two individuals? They were Judas and Silas who, though definitely leaders (see vv. 22, 27), were at that time neither apostles nor elders nor even deacons. We can therefore assert with confidence that the leadership at the local level of the church includes more than elders, although it must certainly be acknowledged that the elders represent the entire leadership of the local assembly.

We can therefore say that for God's house to be set in order there must be present the essential element of leadership. Why is this so? As indicated earlier the church is not a democratically-oriented and arranged entity wherein no or very little leadership is present, thus encouraging the believers in the church to do or say or believe whatever they may wish. There must be leadership in God's house. And though it is quite true that the Lord himself is the Head over the church, He most certainly does delegate His authority to those whom He chooses and makes known as leaders. It is also true that leadership is not, nor is it ever to be, *everything* in the local assembly; nevertheless, it does exercise great influence with regard to whatever progress is made by the church. Indeed, I believe it is commonly acknowledged that if there be strong but good, spiritual and sacrificial leadership in the church, that local assembly is blessed in terms of spiritual growth and progress. On the other hand, if leadership is weak or lacking, that local church will tend to drift aimlessly, with her spiritual direction becoming more and more vague and her growth non-existent. I say, therefore, that leadership is most essential.

A review of Old Testament times will demonstrate that whenever God raised up a good king in the nation of Israel, that nation was highly blessed, but whenever a wicked king arose, the whole nation entered into a period of curse. From this brief historical record regarding Israel we can easily discern the fact that leadership exerts considerable influence, whether that be positive or negative in nature.

I wish to emphasize again that leadership is not the be-all and end-all of everything in God's house. Some Christians have gone to the extreme of making leadership the church: let the leaders decide all things and do all things, with all the rest of the brethren having no part to play in God's house but to merely sit back and enjoy. No, to the contrary, every brother and sister must be a living, functioning member of the church. Every talent must be exercised in the church, not just those talents and gifts possessed by the leadership.

Moreover, it is evident from God's word that the elders are always to be plural in number. And why? Because the Lord himself, being *the* Leader, will not allow one man to be a substitute for Him; He will not permit one single man to represent Him, for there is always the danger of one man becoming a substitute for the Head of the body of Christ. As a precaution, therefore, there is always to be a collective leadership, with the eldership being plural in number. As I trust we have come to see, leadership is very important in the church's growth, but true spiritual leadership is not that which man in and of himself can either appoint or create.

I would here like to quote an insightful passage on leadership which was expressed by J.O. Sanders, who at one time had been the director of the prominent missionary agency in China, the China Inland Mission (CIM):

Spiritual leaders are not made by election or appointment, by man or any combination of man, nor by conference. Only God can make them. Spiritual leadership is a thing of the Spirit and is conferred by God alone. When His searching eye alights on a man who is qualified, He anoints him with His Spirit and separates him to his distinguished ministry. Leadership is not made by man; leadership is chosen by God. In other words, God is sovereign; He sovereignly raises up leadership in the church.

I very much like what Mr. Sanders has expressed about true spiritual leadership. And here I would like to share an incident from the life of the Catholic saint, Francis of Assisi (1181/2-1226), who had been raised up quite sovereignly by God and used greatly by Him. One day a brother in the Franciscan order founded by Francis asked the saint this question: "Why is it that from among all people whom God could choose to use for people to listen to and follow, He chose you? Why is it?" In response Francis, who would at times become ecstatic like a child over something he saw or heard, suddenly began to be full of joy and happiness by what had been asked. Replied the saint: "I'll be happy to tell you why. The eyes of God were searching to and fro throughout the whole earth seeking to find among all the sinners and saints that person who is the most useless and who is the most nothing; and He could not find anyone better than me to match that description. And that is the reason God chose to use me so that no one could boast"!

How so very true, especially when comparing the above words of Francis with that remarkable passage of Paul's in I Corinthians 1:26-28. Too often our thought about leaders is that they are born as leaders, and that they are born with leadership talents. And so we conclude that most certainly such people are destined to be leaders. Yes, in the world that may be so, but with respect to the church and spiritual leadership, that is not true. In comparing the two it would seem that, according to outward appearances, natural leadership and spiritual leadership may sometimes appear to be similar; nevertheless, there are quite a few basic differences between these two types of leadership. And here I would like for us to take note of the many differences which former CIM Director Sanders has so wisely discerned and pointed out:

In natural leadership, invariably the leaders are self-confident, but in spiritual leadership their confidence is in God. In natural leadership the leaders know man; they study human psychology. So they know man, and because they know man and how to maneuver them, they have outward views of them. But spiritual leadership knows God. Natural leadership makes its own decision; therefore, leaders are very decisive. People who are wavering cannot be good leaders. They have to be very decisive and make their own decisions. But spiritual leadership seeks to find God's will. With natural leadership the leaders are ambitious, but spiritual leadership is self-effacing. Natural leadership originates its own method, but spiritual leadership finds and follows God's method. Natural leadership enjoys commanding others; spiritual leadership delights to obey God. Natural leadership is motivated by personal consideration. Spiritual leadership is motivated by love for God and man. Natural leadership is independent; spiritual leadership is God-dependent. Only God appoints leadership.

Then, too, I like what A. W. Tozer wrote about spiritual leadership, which I think is the best analysis, so far as I know, on leadership:

A true and safe leader is likely to be one who has no desire to lead but is forced into a position of leadership by the inward pressure of the Holy Spirit and the press of the external situation. Such were Moses and David and the Old Testament prophets. I think there has not been a great leader from Paul to the present day that was not drafted by the Holy Spirit for the task. Drafted by the Holy Spirit for the task and commissioned by the Lord of the church to fill a position, He had little heart for it. I believe it might be accepted as a fairly reliable rule of thumb that a man who is ambitious to lead is disqualified as a leader. The true leader will have no desire to lord it over God's heritage but will be humble, gentle, self-sacrificing and altogether as ready to follow as to lead when the Spirit makes it clear that the wiser and more gifted man than himself has appeared.

How beautiful and how so very true.

That writing by brother Tozer demonstrates clearly to me the difference between spiritual leadership and natural leadership. Spiritual leadership is raised up by God. If that is the case, then what should be our reaction to this truth? Surely, if spiritual leadership is sovereignly raised up by God, then what must one do? Do you just sit back and wait passively until God raises up spiritual leaders? On the contrary, the truth of God is very well-balanced.

On the one hand, it is true that nobody can make himself or others leaders. When, for example, the apostles appointed elders, they did not do so arbitrarily; they did not appoint them because they liked those particular believers; rather, the apostles appointed them because they had the spiritual discernment to see and understand that the Holy Spirit had manifested certain men as leaders. Hence, they were only recognizing what the Holy Spirit had manifested. It was not an arbitrary appointment on the part of the apostles at all. Nobody can make himself or another person a leader; for it is God who calls; it is God who chooses; it is God who raises up.

On the other hand, this fact does not mean that we should adopt a passive attitude towards this matter; instead, we should pray that the Lord will raise up leaders among His people. Have we therefore really prayed that the Lord would raise up such leaders in our midst locally?

Suppose a group of believers is meeting together and they discover that among them there are no leaders, and that because of this circumstance things are not moving on as they should. What must those believers do? Must they at that point arbitrarily attempt to appoint some as leaders? But if those saints are spiritually knowledgeable and realize that that is not something which should be done, should they be laid back and adopt the attitude of simply deciding to wait until the Lord raises up leaders, and that during this period they should do nothing at all and let the whole church simply drift? Not in the least! We believers have a responsibility to work together with God, so that if we see there is a need for leadership, we should definitely pray that the Head of the house will raise up particular ones as leaders. Moreover, we should not only pray but also move forward in the direction which Paul indicated to Titus when he said, "Appoint elders in every city."

What kind of person should Christian workers like Titus, as guided by the Holy Spirit, look for as those believers in the church who could qualify to be appointed her leaders? As can be seen from the Titus letter's first chapter, the apostle submitted to this young worker a group of qualities or qualifications which was not exhaustive in number but only illustrative in nature. Even so, there are no less than fifteen such qualifications which were put forward by Paul. Why, though, it may be asked, were these qualities for eldership given in Scripture? Two related reasons come to mind here. First, such a list of qualities can serve to assist Christian workers in looking out for those believers in a given local church who in God's eyes are qualified to be her leaders. And, second, I believe this group of qualifications submitted by the apostle to Titus (and also, in similar fashion, to Timothy—see I Timothy 3:1-7) can serve as well in enabling Christian workers to develop those same qualities in the lives of the brethren in the local assembly.

Nevertheless, regardless the reasons God's word has included this set of qualifications for church leadership, it must be clearly recognized by all brethren that determining the leadership for the church is the sole prerogative of God himself and not that which is open to man's opinion or choice. God is the one who decides who should be chosen and raised up as leaders. God reserves this right to himself, yet He never does anything without there being a reason behind His action. And in this matter of leadership, there are certain qualities He is looking to find in some of His people, and whenever those qualities appear in them, only then will He choose them as leaders and make this known by the Holy Spirit to those in the church who are in a position to appoint.

Let me say once more that, firstly, this issue of who is to be a church leader is not a matter to be approached passively; rather, Christian workers are required to labor together with God in this matter. Yes, indeed, it is God who chooses qualified leaders;

but as He makes them known, responsible workers are to pray for the Spirit's guidance and to then be sensitive in their spirit to discern His choice. And, secondly, those who are in a position to help have the responsibility to assist in developing in the lives of brothers in the church those same qualities mentioned in Titus so that they may be considered qualified in God's eyes to be future church leaders. And hence, these two actions and actors in this important undertaking work together.

I firmly believe that Titus was left behind in Crete by Paul for the purpose of accomplishing both these actions. By which I mean that, first, he was to search out among the brothers in the various local assemblies there who might possess these qualifications; and if he should find men who did possess them, he was to appoint those brethren as elders. But, second, were Titus unable to discern any such qualified brothers, then he was to commence developing those qualities in the brothers in the various assemblies on the island. In short, if these qualifications were already evident in brethren, then recognize them as guided by the Spirit and appoint those brothers; but if those qualities were absent, then commence developing them in brothers. An altogether tremendous undertaking, most surely!

As a matter of fact, this was the way the Lord Jesus had raised up leaders in His day. In order to reach the mass, His strategy was to concentrate on the few, which in His case was the Twelve. Hence, in order to build up the church today we need to concentrate on a limited number—on those who demonstrate the potential for exercising church leadership in eventually being used by God to lead the rest of the saints in the right way.

Now in reviewing the set of fifteen qualifications cited in the Titus epistle we will notice that apart from one or two which probably speak of ability or gift (having competence in God's word), the rest are definitely related to character. In choosing leaders in the world, ability is the foremost quality expected to be present and gift is not far behind in importance; however, in the house of God it is not ability but spirituality and it is not gift but grace which are considered to be the foremost qualities in a leader. And we know that spirituality is not a matter of gift but of character. Some brethren in the church are very gifted and they are therefore thought by others to be very spiritual.

This was thought to be true in the church at Corinth. Her brethren were probably the most gifted among all the saints in all the churches at that time. For we will recall how the apostle Paul had described them: "You have been enriched in all the word of doctrine and in all knowledge, you coming short in no gift whatsoever. Moreover, brethren, I have not been able to speak to you as to spiritual but as to fleshly; for you are still carnal" (see I Corinthians 1:5, 7; 3:1a, 3a). We are well acquainted with the fact that the Corinthian church was marked by immense disorder; yet her disorder was not caused by a lack of gifts but by an abundance of gifts whose use they had probably been abusing in a self-gratifying manner. Far from being spiritual, noted the apostle, they had been behaving carnally.

It is instructive to note what this same apostle had observed in Romans 12 when identifying and discussing various gifts, all of which, Paul declared, are according to grace given to us members in the body of Christ. And among the gifts mentioned was that of leadership, which was to be exercised with diligence. Hence, though leadership in the context of Romans 12 is considered a gift that should be exercised with diligence, it is a gift given in accordance with God's grace (see vv. 6, 8c). Therefore, with regard to church leadership's required qualifications, competence in God's word is the only gift cited by Paul in the Titus letter that was included in those qualifications. And thus, it is obvious that gift's percentage of those qualifications is far, far less than that of character. In fact, in reviewing that set of qualifications one finds that it is a well-rounded picture of character.

Let me say something further about Paul's list. There is a tendency for some people to view it as mostly addressing the issue of morality: for example, a leader must be the husband of one wife, must be free of any charge of unseemliness, must not be a winebibber, nor a seeker of gain by dishonest means, and so forth. These obviously are moral and ethical qualities; but here I would like for us to consider the contrast between morality and spirituality as a way of making clearer what I wish to convey; namely, that though there is a difference between these two, it is not to be understood that in being spiritual one can be amoral or immoral or beyond morality. Not so!

Unfortunately, some believers, deeming themselves to be super-spiritual, entertain the mistaken notion that being spiritual they are beyond morality of any kind in their conduct, that because they are spiritual they can behave immorally and it will nonetheless be acceptable in God's sight. Far be this to be true! As a matter of fact, Christian spirituality must *exceed* what morality requires. Otherwise, it would be reasonable and legitimate for the church to appoint as elders any and all of society's so-called good men.

We need to be crystal clear in our understanding that this group of qualifications being discussed here is not to be viewed as expressions of natural morality but they are the result of the Holy Spirit's work of incorporating Christ into the lives of would-be church leaders. In other words, these various qualities in Paul's list are actually the expressions of the character of Christ. To phrase this thought another way, these qualities do not have their source in mankind's fallen Adamic nature but they arise from the new life in Christ which has been developed and is progressively being matured in the lives of those leadership candidates through the Spirit's working in them of the cross; and as a result of all such dealings the character of Christ is being expressed. And that—and nothing else—can be characterized as Christian spirituality.

When viewed from the above-described perspective, how different these qualities put forward by the apostle are from dead-like natural morality; rather, they are the expressions of a living, vibrant spirituality. I would intimate it again that these qualifications cited in the Titus epistle are not to be viewed as the expressions of the so-called good side of fallen Adam; instead, they are the manifestations of the characteristics of Christ's life. And whenever these character traits are developed in the lives of some of God's people and commence making their appearance in them, then it becomes clear that God will choose them to be leaders who shall be set forth as examples to the rest of the saints in His house.

Let us now look somewhat more closely at some of these qualifications for leaders than has been done heretofore. Socially speaking, leaders must, first of all, be beyond all reproach, "as God's steward(s)." They must be free from all charges against themselves. That does not mean, of course, that they are perfect. No one is; nevertheless, in the eyes of society they must possess a good name, reputation and testimony before the observing world, for they are God's stewards or trustees of His mysteries (cf. I Corinthians 4:1). What a tremendous responsibility that is, for should they have some blemish or that which people could hold against them, it would bring disgrace upon the Lord's name.

And morally speaking, a leader must be the husband of one wife. Back in those days many men had more than one wife. Here, therefore, we see that the apostle was setting forth a high standard of moral purity in the marital relationship. Moreover, it is stated that a leader must "not be addicted to wine, not pugnacious, not fond of sordid gain" (NASB). In other words, leaders must be those who physically are self-controlled and are self-disciplined. It is to be understood here that self-discipline and self-control are actually expressions of Spirit-control (Galatians 5:22a, 23a). Those in leadership cannot do whatever their flesh moves them to do: for as God's word tells us, for the Christian, all lusts and passions of the flesh have been crucified with Christ (Galatians 5:24).

Temperamentally, leaders must not be head-strong or passionate; that is, they should not be stubborn or quick-tempered. Mentally, they must be discreet, sensible, just, pious (or, devout), temperate. And domestically speaking, their children are to be believers and who cannot be accused of dissipation or rebellion (NASB).

Last of all, speaking doctrinally, the one in leadership must "cling to the Word, which he can depend on, just as he was taught, so that by sound teaching he can encourage people and correct those who oppose him" (Wm. F. Beck's *New Testament*). This concluding qualification may have more to do with gift or ability than with character.

Even so, it can nonetheless be observed that with regard to all the qualifications which are found in Paul's epistle to Titus, the emphasis is very much on character. Those brethren with the character of Christ in their lives are qualified and will be chosen by God as leaders in the church, and they need to be recognized.

I think one key problem with the church today is that our mind is so democratically-oriented that we think that in all respects everyone is equal. Now in one sense, that is true. In terms of God's grace and life, we are all equal in His sight. In relation to the issue of responsibility, however, there is clearly an order in God's house. For He does set authority in His house. We need to know how to submit ourselves to one another and to those whom God has set above us; and thus a divine order is called for, which needs to be recognized by all believers. We need to recognize Christ in the lives of certain brothers, and in recognizing Him in them, we shall actually be submitting ourselves to Christ and not to those brothers. This is vitally important for all to realize; otherwise, the needful order of God's house cannot be established. Hence, if there is no order present, then it will need to be developed.

One final matter needs to be addressed before concluding our discussion on leadership today. In this letter to Titus there is a great contrast present. In so many words Paul had initially written the following to Titus: "Look for these qualities I have just now outlined, and when you find evidence of them in certain brothers, appoint them as elders because they will be the leaders whom God will have raised up." In reading further on, however, what do we find the situation to be among the believers in Crete? The letter's very first chapter and its verse 10 informs us of the following highly unpleasant, unfortunate circumstance:

For there are many and disorderly vain speakers and deceivers of people's minds, especially those of the circumcision, who must have their mouths stopped, who subvert whole houses, teaching things which ought not to be taught for the sake of base gain. One of themselves, a prophet of their own, has said, Cretans are always liars, evil wild beasts, lazy gluttons.

From history we learn that objective observers of that day praised this prophet for his candor and accurate reporting concerning the citizens of his very own Cretan nation. For in his prophetic writing, he did not spare them of his frank critique: "Cretans are always liars, that they are like evil wild beasts, and are lazy gluttons"! That was not a flattering character assessment in the least. Yet that, in truth, was the actual extremely poor national character of the Cretans back then: they were natural liars, and behaved themselves as though they were evil wild beasts. In other words, whenever Cretans wanted to get something for themselves, they were ruthless in their conduct in doing so; they did not in the least care if other people suffered as a consequence so long as they could obtain what they wanted. Moreover, Cretans in general were very lazy and gluttonous.

These, then, were the natural personality- and behavioral-traits of the island's population; but added to all of these dispiriting aspects of the Cretan national character was the fact that among the many Jews who over time had settled in Crete were some Judaizing members of the circumcision party who had begun teaching the native population on the island those things, noted the apostle, "which ought not to be taught." In fact, Paul continued, these Judaizers were found subverting entire Cretan households with their unscriptural teachings—and doing so, reported Paul to Titus, "for the sake of base gain." Furthermore, he went on to say these same Judaizers, whose teaching content contained numerous fables about Moses, Elijah, and different aspects of Jewish history and culture, sought to deceive their fellow citizens on the island by "turning their minds to Jewish fables and commandments of men" in an attempt to "turn them away from the truth."

In this very regard, we may recall that the apostle, having left Timothy at Ephesus, had instructed him to warn "some" there, who were themselves teaching myths, fables, and endless genealogies, to cease doing so (I Timothy 1:3-4, 4:1 ff.). Among the Cretans, however, there were not merely "some" but "many" who, like those in Ephesus, were "disorderly vain speakers and deceivers of people's minds" and who, accordingly, wrote Paul, "must have their mouths stopped."

Thus were joined together a most wicked and morally destructive combination composed of, first, a people who possessed an extremely unflattering national character and, second, a most deceitful, confusion-spreading group of Judaizers. It should therefore come as no surprise that the coming together of these two elements was what made the Cretans what they were.

With such a background as this, it would be no exaggeration in the slightest for me to observe that the Cretans had a real and immense moral and spiritual problem. Nevertheless, we can thank God that many of them were saved. Even so, it was not going to be easy for their character to be transformed.

On the one hand, though, this highly challenging set of circumstances back then demonstrated the power and glory of the gospel of Jesus Christ, in that, despite what the Cretans were, God, by means of that gospel, had redeemed many of them and was even now looking for some who by the time of Paul's and Titus's visits there had definitely come into possession of a sterling character. Is that not marvelous in terms of what the good news of the Lord Jesus and God's grace could do in saving and considerably transforming quite a few of these Cretans, and even, further, in making some of them qualified to be leaders in God's house! How wonderful that because these redeemed Cretans now had Christ in them—"Christ in us the hope of glory" (see Colossians 1:27b)—God could justifiably be looking for the maturing Christ-character in them. How most wonderful, indeed!

Yes, on the one hand, here was the power and glory of the gospel being demonstrated for all to behold. On the other hand, it must be stated in all candor that among many others of this island's saved population there were extremely serious problems and difficulties which required a great amount of time and perseverance to correct, and to make possible the development and maturing of the embryonic stage of the Christ-character that was definitely already in them. Which clearly explains why the apostle Paul himself could not complete this task and why, for that matter, neither could Titus do so within the period of time he had remained in Crete till summoned by the apostle to join him at Nicopolis for the winter. It requires a great deal of time, indeed, to develop and progressively mature Christ's character in believers; but let us thank God that even in our own day that character can and will be developed among the brethren in God's house today if those of us who may be in a position to be His instruments in effecting that development are faithful and diligent.

In conclusion, I need to express my sincere hope that in our reading together today from God's word of these many unfortunate dire circumstances which were present everywhere among God's people in Crete it will not plunge us into even a modicum of despair, we ending up thinking that if a less dire situation be the case anywhere in the church in our own day, who can be a leader? Who is competent for such a challenging task? Certainly I, too, must acknowledge that in and of myself I am not qualified, nor am I competent. Indeed, none of us is qualified or competent. Nevertheless, as Paul once declared, our competence lies not in us but in God himself (II Corinthians 3:5), and He it is who by His grace and power can qualify us.

God can accomplish this needful undertaking if we are willing to cooperate with Him in allowing the Holy Spirit to do His transforming work of incorporating more of the Christ-character in us by means of the cross being brought to bear upon our self-life. For actually, the fundamental qualification for church leadership is nothing less than the character of Christ. Talents and/or abilities can be helpful, but they are not basic in the development of leadership.

May God raise up leaders in every local assembly, leaders whom He has called and has equipped and who are willing to give themselves sacrificially to the Lord and to His people. For when once such leadership is present, the house of God can be set in order. May God by His mercy and grace help us.

Our heavenly Father, how we praise and thank Thee that Thou art the One who is the Leader in the church and that Thou dost equip and qualify some of the saints to be leaders of Thy people. Actually it is Thou thyself in them who leads. So we do pray that we all may desire to work together with Thee in Thy work of building the house of God. Oh, we pray that Thou wilt raise up leaders for Thy people. We pray that Thou wilt work in the lives of Thy people in such a way that Christ may be manifested, recognized and followed. We want Thy church to be set in order. In the name of our Lord Jesus. Amen.

Chapter Three

Setting God's House in Order: Discipline

Titus 1:10-16—For there are many and disorderly vain speakers and deceivers of people's minds, specially those of the circumcision, who must have their mouths stopped, who subvert whole houses, teaching things which ought not to be taught for the sake of base gain. One of themselves, a prophet of their own, has said, Cretans are always liars, evil wild beasts, lazy gluttons. This testimony is true; for which cause rebuke them severely, that they may be sound in the faith, not turning their minds to Jewish fables and commandments of men turning away from the truth. All things are pure to the pure; but to the defiled and unbelieving nothing is pure; but both their mind and their conscience are defiled. They profess to know God, but in works deny him, being abominable, and disobedient, and found worthless as to every good work.

Titus 3:10-11—An heretical man after a first and second admonition have done with, knowing that such a one is perverted, and sins, being self-condemned.

It was mentioned before that this young man Titus was a person who had been well-disciplined by the Lord and who possessed a sterling Christian character; and that because of this, he was in a position to be used by God to help solve difficult problems confronting various local churches. For instance, we have noted that the apostle Paul had left him behind in Crete for the express purpose of putting the house of God in order there.

Moreover, it has been pointed out previously that if God's house is to be set in order, then according to Paul's letter to Titus, there must be present in His house at least four essential elements, those four being: leadership, discipline, sound teaching, and good works. All of them are equally important—even vital—in the work of setting the house of God in order. And should any one of these elements be lacking, it is doubtful if God's house can be built.

Now during our last time together the first of these four, that of leadership, was discussed at some length. And I trust that through that discussion we came to realize that if the house of God is to be put in proper order, local church leaders must be raised up and chosen by God, then recognized by those in a position to discern, and ultimately be established by their being appointed and by their commencing to function.

Today I would like for us to consider the second element for setting God's house in order: discipline. For this we find the apostle emphasizing as well in his letter written to Titus. Unfortunately, I fear that at the mere mention of that word discipline, the reaction on the part of some, and perhaps many, of God's people will be rejection or even hostility. Sad to say, this term discipline is very much misunderstood, but is also a description of action which has been greatly abused. And because of those regretful circumstances, there has developed over the years an instinctive fear bordering on hostility among many of God's people towards this subject of discipline, it resulting in their thinking that to be free from discipline is to know and experience true freedom in the Lord. Actually, however, it is through discipline that we are truly made free; for the person who lacks discipline in his or her life is a person in bondage, whereas the person who experiences discipline is free *not* to do what he or she should not do and is able to *do* what should be done. Consequently, this latter person is truly free.

Allow me to say at the very outset of our discussion together today concerning discipline that an undisciplined person is not a mature individual. Only through discipline can character be developed and hence, only the person who is under discipline will be in a position to be used by God. This is not only true individually among God's people but also true corporately as members together of the body of Christ, the church. Without the element of discipline in the church there can be no order therein; and if there be no order present therein, there is no church. Therefore, it can legitimately be stated that an assembly of God's people which is without discipline is not a church. In other words, there can be no reality of the church until there is the reality of discipline present.

The Old Testament book of Proverbs, which is a book of wisdom, is full of passages on this subject of discipline. We shall notice in those passages that different words have been employed to describe the idea of discipline—such terms as instruction, admonition, reproof, chastening, correction, and rod. Nevertheless, in considering all these passages together, there is but one idea, notion or concept which is constantly being expressed or conveyed, and it is quite obviously that of discipline. Let us notice below just a few of these passages by chapter and verse or verses, and that are each accompanied by a brief comment of mine.

3:11-12: "My son, despise not the instruction of Jehovah, neither be weary of his chastisement; for whom Jehovah loveth he chasteneth, even as a father the son in whom he delightest." These words convey to us the thought of discipline, and let us recall that they are quoted in the New Testament book of Hebrews (see 12:5-6).

6:23: "For the commandment is a lamp, and the teaching a light, and reproofs of instruction are the way of life." Reproofs by means of instruction is another way of speaking of discipline, and such reproofs are the way of life.

12:1: "Whoso loveth discipline loveth knowledge, but he that hateth reproof is brutish." I think this brief succinct message on discipline is very clear.

13:24: "He that spareth his rod hateth his son; but he that loveth him chasteneth him betimes." This is a saying of which I believe most parents are aware and understand.

There are many other passages in Proverbs which deal with discipline; and their high number is evidence of how important discipline is in our lives! Perhaps you dislike the term discipline (or its synonym, chastening), but this term actually means, and has reference to the more innocent-sounding term of, what is called child-training. We may therefore conclude that involved in child-training are such things as instruction, correction, admonition and warning. And they are conveyed to the child verbally or else administered or applied by means of some concrete action on the part of the parent. Without such forms of training—and regardless the terms one wishes to employ to describe the means by which to effect the training—a child will never be able to grow into manhood or womanhood. Discipline in the form of child-training is therefore a must.

This is not only true in the physical human sense; it is likewise true spiritually among the Lord's people. Any child of God who hates discipline and seeks to avoid it may not suffer in that circumstance, but that one will not be able to grow into the mature man or woman of God. Furthermore, without the discipline of spiritual child-training, the child of God will never experience the inner development of Christ's character which is so necessary for being knit together with others in the building up of the church as the house of God.

Hebrews 12 says that our God is our Father who treats us as sons and not as illegitimate offspring. Because of that He chastens us—that is, He disciplines or child-trains us—in order that we may be made partakers of His divine character in terms of His righteousness and holiness (vv. 7-10). Individually and spiritually we each need His discipline, and thank God that the Father knows how and when to discipline us. Sometimes we hear expressed the phrase, "the discipline of the Holy Spirit," but that phrase is not to be found in God's word. Even so, that phrase does convey a bit of Biblical truth. What do I mean by saying this? Well, there are times when the Holy Spirit will arrange our circumstances in order that we may be disciplined and trained not by the Spirit but by our Father-God whose task it is to do the disciplining, for He knows how and when to implement it in our lives. On the other hand, it is the Holy Spirit's responsibility to arrange our circumstances in such a manner that we are given occasions and opportunities to be disciplined by our Father; but as the writer of Hebrews has made clear, our problem is that we often despise our Father's chastening and at times we even faint under His discipline. Nevertheless, the Father's discipline is necessary.

Though as just now pointed out personal discipline by our Father-God is necessary for the Christ-character to be developed and matured in the inner life of the individual believer, I shall not be addressing any further today that particular aspect of the spiritual life among God's people but instead we shall be considering together the discipline which must be present in the house of God. It is quite true, of course, that personal individual discipline is most essential to one's spiritual growth and the development of one's spiritual character. Then, once each and all individual believers who have experienced the Father's personal discipline are put together as the corporate vessel of God, they become, as it were, living stones that are to be built up into a spiritual house, even a holy habitation of God in the Spirit (I Peter 2:5; Ephesians 2:19, 21-22). Such believers will thus discern immediately the vital importance of discipline in God's house, because they have experienced their own personal discipline and how it had helped them immensely. Henceforth today, therefore, we shall be concentrating on the essential element of discipline in the house of God and the proper manner with which it is to be exercised. For if there is no discipline present or if it be wrongfully administered, how can God's house be built? It will instead be plagued by disorder and chaos, and the undertaking will end in failure.

As an example of such resultant disorder, let us look somewhat closely at the church in Corinth. Her members were rich both in knowledge and in gifts; and yet, that church was seemingly very reluctant to exercise *any* form of discipline. They considered themselves so loving and so liberal-minded that after a brother in their midst had committed a sin which was rarely seen even in the world, the church brethren would not deal with that brother. They addressed the matter, if at all, as though the gross immorality had never happened. Indeed, these Corinthian brethren had probably even boasted of how liberal-minded they were and consequently, the Corinthian church displayed a complete lack of discipline in the matter.

When the apostle Paul, who was not in Corinth at the time, heard of this incident, he was stirred by the Holy Spirit to write them as follows: "You must deal with that person. For the time being, remove that wicked man from among yourselves. Do you not know that a little leaven will leaven the whole lump of dough? Purge out the old leaven from your midst so that you may be a fresh new lump of unleavened bread before God" (see I Corinthians 5:1-8, 13b).

How important it is for the church to have discipline, especially in the case of the churches on the island of Crete. Why do I say that about the Cretan assemblies of believers? It is because, given the natural characteristics of the Cretan population in general—they being constant liars, were behaving like evil wild beasts, were fearsome, ruthless and brutal, as well as they were lazy and gluttonous—combined as those morally and socially unacceptable traits were with the deceitful, conniving conduct being perpetrated by the Judaizers numbered among the circumcision party of the Jews who over time had settled on the island, it had become quite clear to the apostle Paul that the exercise of discipline—even of a strong kind—was greatly called for and necessary.

Before proceeding any further, therefore, I need to have us consider more closely than heretofore these Cretan Judaizers who were teaching some, perhaps many, of God's people in Crete those things which should not be taught.

First of all, it should be understood that there was a difference between these Judaizers in Crete and the ones who constantly followed Paul wherever he traveled in Asia Minor, Macedonia, and other geographical areas in the Roman Empire prior to his having been taken a captive to Rome. Those Judaizers had followed Paul everywhere in an attempt to confuse the gospel message which he consistently preached in every place he visited and ministered the pure gospel of the Lord Jesus. However, though these earlier Judaizers who had troubled Paul were Christians who had believed in Christ, they were nonetheless strict Jewish disciples of the Mosaic Law. They greatly emphasized keeping that Law, especially the rite of circumcision. Hence, they had wished to mix Judaism and the Christian gospel together—that is to say, they had fervently desired to Judaize the Christian faith.

In contrast with those Judaizers with whom the apostle had to contend continually elsewhere in the Roman Empire, the Judaizers on the isle of Crete were a different breed. They, too, taught on circumcision, but they were not strict Law-keepers. Rather, their primary interests lay in Jewish fables, the teachings and commandments of men—even the many traditions of man which various religious leaders in

Judaism had over the centuries concocted—and other notions of that sort.

Furthermore, these Cretan Judaizers had mixed all the aforementioned beliefs, teachings and errant notions with several well-developed human philosophies of that day, along with some aspects of mysticism, endless genealogies, and other non-Christian ideas. They had even begun to dabble in Gnosticism which at this time had not been well-developed yet, but there were the beginnings already of various speculations which would later become solidified together into an influential Gnostic philosophy in competition with the true Christian gospel. These Judaizers, therefore, full as they were with all sorts of unwarranted speculations, arguments and reasonings, had over time become dangerous and hurtful deceivers of many Cretans' minds—including the minds of many Christians on the island. In short, these Judaizers in Crete were a far worse type than those who had constantly troubled Paul everywhere he went.

As a consequence of all these unfortunate developments, it is not to be wondered at that in the local churches throughout the island there had arisen, as the apostle had noted with alarm in his Titus epistle, many disorderly vain speakers, false prophets and false teachers. They were continually putting forth in their teachings various ideas and beliefs of theirs which, declared Paul to Titus, ought not to be taught, especially because in addition they were doing so for the sake of sordid gain financially;

and, it could be further added, even also, perhaps, for the sake of accruing to themselves some fame, popularity, and/or followers.

These developments constituted real problems and posed serious challenges for the Cretan churches. This was because through their much vain speaking and false teaching these Judaizers, together with those false teachers and false prophets who had also made their appearance in the Cretan churches, were leading the saints away from the truth of Christ's gospel.

Yet, not only were these Judaizers and the others causing many of the saints to turn their backs on that essential truth; they were also causing disunity within the church, in that as a result of their extremely unsound speaking and teaching, God's people were beginning to divide into factions or sects. This we learn from Paul at nearly the very end of the letter of instructions to Titus. For there in verse 10 of chapter 3 the apostle uses a descriptive phrase in referring generically to a particular class or group of people whose words and actions create division. The phrase in question, translated in Darby's Bible version, is: "an heretical man," which is to say that such a man speaks forth heresy. And the factious class or group of people whom Paul had in mind in employing this phrase was all those many troublemakers he had identified and described earlier in his epistle.

Now before proceeding further in considering this phrase of Paul's, it may be helpful in that regard to provide a little historical background on the meaning of the word heresy and its adjectival form, heretical. When this word heresy came into use in relation to the Christian faith and church, the meaning intended to be conveyed by its use was quite different from what it has come to mean or convey in our day. When we say today that something being taught is heresy or heretical, we mean that what is being presented is a false belief, teaching or doctrine which is contrary to that which is generally accepted as true Christian orthodoxy.

In its original use, however, the word heresy simply meant "that which one chooses for himself, an opinion." And over time the adoption and/or advocacy of a particular opinion or series of opinions had developed into a school of opinion(s) formally recognized as constituting a group of people who espoused and promulgated a number of particular opinions—opinions which might have been contrary to what was generally accepted by the intelligentsia and/or society of that day and time. And thus, if applied to the church, the word heresy back then eventually took on the meaning of faction or sect or party, the term having therefore taken on a sinister, perhaps even an evil, meaning in relation to the Christian church.

Which brings us back to Paul's descriptive phrase he had employed in Titus 3:10 to further describe, beyond what he had laid out initially in his epistle, all those various troublemakers who were causing serious problems for the Cretan churches. As was noted a few moments ago, that phrase in Darby is translated as "an heretical man." If we consult several other Bible translations of Titus 3:10, we can arrive at a fuller and clearer understanding of the meaning of this phrase back then as it had pertained, in particular, to the Christian church: "a man who chooses to be different in his teaching" (Beck), "a factious man" (NASB), and "a divisive person" (NIV). Hence, we come to understand, in Paul's thinking, what kind of persons these heretical men were in that earlier period of the church.

They were those who without any basis or justification had chosen to adopt for themselves certain opinions and ideas which were different from true church teachings. And having adopted those errant opinions and notions for themselves, they had then commenced propagating them among God's people wherever assembled Christians were to be found. And from reviewing again the entire Titus letter, we can correctly assume that the nature, content or substance of those opinions and ideas which the heretical men of that day *in Crete* had grasped hold of, espoused, and were disseminating widely was a mixture together of various Jewish fables and myths, numerous human-originated commandments, unprofitable and worthless genealogies, and a variety of foolish Gnostic arguments and speculations. A hodgepodge mixture, indeed!

As a consequence of their much vain talk and teaching, however, there began to appear factions or parties among the believers in Crete. These in turn were creating controversy, strife and, ultimately, divisions in the church and causing the breaking up of

God's house on the island. Undeniably, the local expressions of the body of Christ there had fallen into great disorder—even, one could say, chaos.

Now because of this disorder and chaos, there was clearly a great need for discipline if the churches in Crete were to be set in order. And in view of the need for that essential element to be established, there can be found among the apostle Paul's many and varied instructions to Titus a considerable emphasis on discipline. For how is one to deal with a church situation in which, as Paul explained, "there are many and disorderly vain speakers and deceivers of people's minds" at work throughout the various local expressions of God's house in Crete? It was evident, the apostle believed, that the discipline needing to be applied must be quite strong, since he instructed Titus that the mouths of these workers of disorder and discord "must be stopped"—a very strong word of disciplinary action, indeed, because the word stopped literally means "to be made dead"!

It must be acknowledged, of course, that within certain limits, people in general have agreed that there is the principle and practice of the freedom of speech. If, at a church meeting, for example, the Lord gives someone a word to share, that person is free to do so. However, there is no such principle and practice in the church, as one Christian brother once observed, of someone having the freedom of engaging in misleading speech. Supposed, for instance, someone rises up in a church meeting and begins sharing some nonsensical notion or errant speculation or false teaching whose words are meant to deceive the listeners' minds. Does that person have the freedom to put forth misleading, even untruthful, speech? On the contrary, instructed Paul, You, Titus, must rise up and, as it were, totally deaden that one's mouth; that person's speech, Titus, must be entirely silenced. That is strong discipline. Dare we do that today? Can we do that? This apostle of the Lord said, Yes, you *must* do that.

Moreover, throughout his letter to Titus, the apostle can be found using some very strong language in indicating the kind of stringent discipline which might be called for in certain church situations. In Titus 1:13 and Titus 2:15, for example, Paul tells his younger co-worker to "rebuke them severely" and "rebuke with all authority" those in the church who would need to be dealt with severely, if necessary. As a further example of Paul's insistence on exercising strong, severe discipline if required, I must have us again return to a consideration of Titus 3:10-11, where Paul is found advising Titus in the severest language how "an heretical man" must be disciplined. Speaking in singular number but referencing generically all those troublemaking heretical men who were discussed earlier today, the apostle declared the following with regard to how one must deal with such factious workers of disunity in the Cretan churches: "Warn a divisive person once, and then warn them a second time. After that, have nothing to do with them. You may be sure that such people are warped and sinful; they are self-condemned" (NIV). That is in fact very severe discipline.

We may wonder why it was necessary that such drastic forms of discipline be meted out. It was because the situation in the Cretan churches was so seriously flawed, disordered and chaotic that it demanded strong and severe discipline for the sake of restoring the unity of the body of Christ, for the sake further of preventing God's people from any longer being led away from the truth, and thus also for the sake of ensuring the building of the house of God. It was not for any selfish reason but for these reasons alone that Paul's series of strong forms of discipline had to be applied. And, it may be observed, Titus was the right person in the right place and at the right time to continue the apostle's initiated but unfinished work of setting God's house in order via the application of necessary discipline.

An undisciplined person would not be fit to exercise discipline. Furthermore, even if he should try, nobody would pay him any heed, and it would therefore not be effective in the least. However, here was a young man who was a highly disciplined person and who was thus qualified to exercise discipline in setting God's house in order in Crete. And so, it follows, then, that the brothers who would be raised up by God, and subsequently recognized and appointed by a Titus or a Paul, would themselves eventually be those to exercise discipline in the Cretan local churches. And because of that circumstance, how highly disciplined personally those future elders must likewise be!

Now we will recall that among the qualifications for eldership there are these: they must be discreet, just, pious, temperate, with their temper under control; in other words, they must be highly disciplined. Unless they themselves are disciplined, how can they discipline any disorderly believers who will be under their care? Those in the position of leadership have to exercise discipline, and that is why they themselves must be disciplined. Because there is no perfect *person* in the world except the Lord Jesus, those of us who may be elevated by God to be in leadership in the church need to be disciplined first.

Then, too, there is no perfect *church* in the world. Some of God's people are continually looking unsuccessfully for a perfect church—I have met a few. As one brother has observed concerning such people, "They are spiritual butterflies." Unfortunately, because they could not find that perfect church in their searching, they are never committed to anything. Let us recognize the fact that since there is no perfect church on earth there shall always be the need for discipline. Your church situation may not be as bad as that of the churches in Crete, or it may be that it could be worse; nevertheless, it must be acknowledged that in the experience of every assembly of God's people this matter of discipline will sooner or later need to be addressed.

The question therefore arises, How is the church going to handle the exercise of discipline? If she simply overlooks the issue completely by allowing its lack to run its course, the church will become disorderly and not grow, with all kinds of problems arising. Or suppose those in the church do exercise discipline but do so with a wrong spirit or in the wrong way; that could actually split the church and cause more problems. It thus becomes evident that the essential element of discipline and how it is to be exercised in the local church poses a real challenge in the building of God's house. On the one hand, without discipline there will be no order, and without order there can be no testimony of the church. On the other hand, the handling of discipline is such a difficult and delicate responsibility that those in the church who must carry it out are at times truly afraid to be involved in implementing discipline when necessary. Especially is this true for those who know what discipline entails because they themselves have experienced the Lord's discipline. Hence, they are very reluctant to exercise discipline.

Permit me here to quote what J. N. Darby has written on this subject of exercising discipline in the church:

> We ought to remember what we are in ourselves when we talk about exercising discipline. It is an amazingly solemn thing. When I reflect that I am a poor sinner, saved by mercy, standing only in Jesus Christ for acceptance, in myself vile, it is evidently an awesome thing to take discipline into my hands. Who can judge, save God? This

is my first thought. Only one thing gets me over that feeling and that is, the prerogative of love. When love is really exercised, it cares for nothing but the accomplishment of its object. Though the subject matter of conduct be righteous, that which sets it going is love. Love is exercised to secure at all costs of pain to itself the blessing of holiness in the church. It is not a position of superiority in the flesh.

How true it is what brother Darby has said here. That when he considers who he is—a poor vile sinner saved by God's mercy and only now, being clothed with Christ as his righteousness, could he have ever been accepted by God—how, then, can he judge anybody in the church and exercise discipline because of some error or misbehavior on that person's part? Mr. Darby concludes that the only thing which enables him to overcome that sense of unworthiness in being the one to discipline any fellow church member is "the prerogative of love." If, states brother Darby in so many words, you are filled with love and your love for your brother is such that you are willing to go through a painful process in order to reach that brother and restore him, that is the only way anyone can exercise discipline in God's house.

I think that is the right spirit to have in approaching this responsibility of exercising discipline. Who actually are we? If we really know ourselves, we must confess that we are merely poor sinners saved by grace and who can now stand before God only because we have been clothed with Jesus Christ as our righteousness (Romans 13:14, Galatians 3:27, I Corinthians 1:30, II Corinthians 5:21). For us who were poor vile sinners but have been saved by God's grace to take up discipline into our hands is hence an incredibly awesome undertaking.

Now in approaching this element of discipline so essential in the life of the church, according to God's word, there appear to be three different kinds—and perhaps it can be said that there are three different stages—of discipline. The first kind of discipline to be exercised among God's people is that pertaining to brotherly relationships, and it is described in Matthew 18:15-17. There we read what Jesus had said to His disciples concerning this matter:

> ... if thy brother sin against thee, go, reprove him between thee and him alone. If he hear thee, thou hast gained thy brother. But if he do not hear thee, take with thee one or two besides, that every matter may stand upon the word of two witnesses or of three. But if he will not listen to them, tell it to the [church]; and if also he will not listen to the [church], let him be to thee as one of the nations and a tax-gatherer.

Jesus' opening words on this subject are quite simple: "If a brother sins against you." We recognize, of course, that such a circumstance can easily happen within the context of a local assembly where "two or three" brethren meet together (see v.20). And because these brethren are in such close proximity to each other as members one of another, there is bound to be frequent opportunity for one brother to sin against another.

We can perhaps liken this circumstance to the relationship which existed between two of Jesus' twelve disciples who happened to be flesh-and-blood brothers. And because of being brethren in the flesh, these two—Peter and Andrew—were naturally thrown together quite often in life; so much so that it would have been very easy for one of them to sin against the other, and vice versa. Let us notice, however, that though Andrew, as far as we know, never complained to the Lord, Peter did. Said he to the Master: "Lord, my brother sinned against me seven times, and each time I forgave him" (see v.21).

Given Peter's impulsive, quick-tempered, impatient personality, more than likely he at this moment must have been extremely happy with himself for having patiently endured his brother's trespasses against him seven consecutive times without once having exploded into anger towards his brother, whom instead he had each time forgiven. For Peter that was quite an achievement.

However, though Peter probably came to Jesus in a happy frame of mind over what he had accomplished, he nonetheless believed there should be a limit to his forgiving; for he complained to the Lord as follows: "I forgave my brother these seven times. Is not seven times enough?" Indeed, this disciple probably expected the Lord to say in response: "Yes, Peter, that was very good of you. It most certainly *is* enough." As we well know, of course, Jesus had responded otherwise.

There is one aspect to this incident about which I have often wondered: Though it was Peter who had complained that his brother Andrew had sinned against him, *who*—I have asked myself—actually had been doing the sinning? For I believe Andrew was a very careful person who was observant of even the smallest of things. As but one example of this trait in him, let us take note of the small but significant role he played on the occasion of Jesus' feeding of the 5,000 men, along with the many women and children who were also present—it thus perhaps being some 10,000 people who had gathered together to hear the Lord teach. And in going through this immense crowd of people Andrew had noticed that a boy had brought for himself a small meal consisting of five barley loaves and two fish. But he added in his reporting of this discovery to the Lord, "What is this small amount of food for so many hungry people" (see John 6:8-9)? This incident is an indication of how observant and careful Andrew was on this occasion, and probably he was this very same way most of the time in his life. Would he not therefore have naturally been careful as well in his relationship with his brother by having avoided the committing of a trespass against his brother?

This is why I have wondered who between these two brothers was really the one who had sinned against the other. Given Peter's impulsive, quick-tempered and impatient behavior at times, perhaps he had simply gotten angry at something and flew into a rage, he subsequently projecting onto Andrew his incorrect belief that it was his brother Andrew who was guilty of having done that which had triggered Peter's anger and rage. For it is sometimes the one who is doing the sinning who ends up being the one who complains.

God has put us together, but if, as someone has observed, we could place an arm's length of space between ourselves and our brother or sister, we could live much more peacefully together. In that case, however, God's house would never be built. He has put us together as members of the one body of Christ, the church. He has put two or more of us in the same place and who have gathered together to the name of the Lord (see again Matthew 18:20). And being together in this manner there will doubtless be numerous instances of someone sinning against another, stepping upon another, offending another. But when such things happen, what is to be done?

Back in the time of the Mosaic Law, the governing code of conduct was: "An eye for an eye, tooth for tooth, hand for hand, foot for foot," even also "life for life" (see Exodus 21:23-24). Which meant that if someone happened to take out one of your eyes you had the right to remove one of his eyes, and so on. But for us in the church, being Christians, what is to be the proper reaction? We most certainly cannot in return take revenge; but the inward attitude we might actually adopt may not be any better, since we might say to ourselves: "Unfortunately, because I am a Christian, I must endure the injury which has been inflicted upon me—whether I am willing or not, for I am well aware that the Lord, in His response to Peter, declared that it was not to be merely seven times a person is to forgive an offender but seventy times seven: a seemingly infinite number! (Matthew 18:22); and hence, I am irrevocably trapped and must regrettably accept what has been done to me without any payback being rendered in return." And further, even though we may say to the offending brother or sister, "I forgive you," but we do not forget what we have supposedly forgiven, can any of us claim that the forgiveness extended was rendered from the heart? For the Christian standard to be observed is what in so many words the Lord Jesus had declared: "My heavenly Father shall not forgive you if you do not forgive your brother (or sister) from your heart" (see Matthew 18:35).

Recently I have been meditating on the so-called Lord's prayer. Using William Beck's translation, *The New Testament in the Language of Today*, it reads in part as follows: "And forgive us our sins as we have forgiven those who sin against us" (Matthew 6:12). If we really know what that means, probably we dare not pray this part of the prayer. In this connection, the story is told that when the great English Bible expositor, G. Campbell Morgan, spoke publicly on this verse, a lady who heard him wrote him a letter of inquiry: "Is it all right when I pray this prayer—and this has been my practice—that I may change it somewhat? For I pray (she adapting her prayer from the Authorized or King James Version's text), "Forgive us our debt and we will forgive our debtors." Of course, Campbell Morgan wrote back, saying: "You cannot do that."

Let us meditate for a moment on this prayer passage, it being directed towards the Father in heaven: "Forgive us our sins as we have forgiven those who sin against us." This is as much as saying that if we do not forgive from the heart those who sin against us, as Jesus had himself explained, then our Father will not forgive us. Please be advised that this is not a sinner's prayer. A sinner's prayer would be: "Oh God, forgive me," and He in response forgives. No, what is being discussed here is the prayer of the church. After we, by God's grace and mercy, have had our sins forgiven for salvation, we ought to manifest the character of our Lord Jesus, which is that we forgive those who sin against us from the heart, and on that basis the Father forgives us. This is very important for us to understand and genuinely put into practice in our Christian walk—it is very important.

With all that as an initial background, let us return to Jesus' disciple Simon Peter and his interaction with the Lord concerning this spiritual exercise called forgiveness.

Peter, in coming to the Lord, said, "I forgave my brother seven times." Excuse me, dear brethren, but if you have counted and kept a record in your mind on how many times you have forgiven your brother, then I have to wonder how much forgiveness you have actually extended towards your brother. If you know and remember the number of times you have said to him, "I forgive you," then I would surmise that the amount is not very much, if any! For it is indicative to me that in your having kept a record, you have not forgotten, and if not forgotten, then most likely no forgiveness from the heart has taken place, since that requires forgiving *and* forgetting.

Not only must you forgive and forget, says the Lord Jesus, but He takes this matter one step further, it in its entirety touching on the first kind or stage of discipline that is to be exercised in the church. For He said to His disciples: "If your brother has sinned against you, you must go to him in private—just the two of you alone. Show him where he has wronged you" (see Matthew 18:15a).

Regrettably, too often that is not what actually happens in today's church. If, for instance, a brother should sin against me, the more likely response on my part will be that I shall silently say to myself, "The offense is not that serious, so I shall let it go." Furthermore, by my not speaking up, or if I should gossip to others behind that brother's back about what he did towards me, I may perhaps find welling up within me a sense of victory having been achieved over that brother, which will make me feel good and shall compensate me somewhat for the pain and injury I have suffered at the hands of that brother! However, the Lord Jesus would react to such conduct of mine with great disappointment bordering on utter disgust; for He would declare in no uncertain terms, "That is *not* the right response in the least; there must be discipline involved in such a situation, and *you* as the offended party must be the one to exercise it for the sake of that offending brother's restoration." We can thus see here how badly the church of God is failing to manifest this first kind of discipline in her midst.

(Of course, it should be pointed out that if it is the case that it is you who has sinned against your brother, doubtless what is required is that you must go to that brother and humbly and sincerely apologize.)

It would be well to pause here, for there are a few additional observations which ought to be made concerning the situation of a brother who has sinned against you. If this should happen to you, you are never to wait for that offending brother to come to you and apologize. The Lord would say "No" to that kind of reaction of yours as well. For most likely that brother is in spiritual darkness and will probably never come to you. Instead, because you are in the *light*, you must go to *him*; and by the very act of your going, it should mean that you have already forgiven him completely and have been praying for him. And thus, you will not be going to him in a spirit of revenge or of seeking to vindicate yourself in his eyes, but you will be going to him, as brother Darby has pointed out, in the spirit of love.

Yes, it is true that I have suffered as a consequence of my brother having sinned against me; but that is nothing; I am willing to suffer till my brother has been restored. For when I contemplate the thought that my brother is in spiritual darkness, that means his communion and fellowship both with the Lord and with the brothers and sisters have suffered. And hence, what a loss my brother is experiencing. I must be used by the Lord to restore him to full spiritual health. I must therefore go to him. Now if that is how this kind of situation plays itself out, then it can rightly be said that discipline of the brotherly relationship type is truly being exercised in God's house.

Accordingly, the first kind of discipline which needs to be carried out among God's people in the church is that having to do with brotherly (or, as the case may be, sisterly, or brotherly-sisterly, or sisterly-brotherly) relationships. It is because you yourself have been disciplined by our heavenly Father that you therefore have the responsibility to seek out and discipline your erring brother (or sister). However, this discipline is not to be expressed by your saying to him something along the line of the following: "Do you not realize, my brother, that you have committed this trespass towards me?" No, your speaking to him should not be expressed with that kind of spirit. Rather, you should attempt to show him that what he has done will hinder not only his life with the Lord but also his life with the other church brethren and with you. In addition, it should be made clear to your brother that your coming and speaking to him is not for your sake but for his good—for his spiritual well-being.

Let us all realize that whatever trespass any of us may commit towards another member in the church will hinder the building of God's house. If, therefore, a brother sins against you, you must go to him for the purpose of restoring him so that nothing of this nature will stand in the way of the building of the house of God. Hence, the discipline which you must carry out towards an offending brother or sister is to be done in the spirit of love and concern for the sake of his or her restoration and never to be exercised for the sake of punishment. Whenever God disciplines us, He is not doing so to punish us. Unfortunately, many believers have that mistaken notion; indeed, I have met and talked with some saints who have said, "God has punished me." To which I would respond by saying: "No, God is disciplining, child-training and chastising you in order to restore you." Discipline is always for restoration, and therefore, in this area of brotherly (or, sisterly) relationships, if you have been sinned against by your brother, you will need to go to him and try to restore him to good spiritual health.

Suppose, however, despite your best efforts in having sought to restore the brother who has wronged you, he does not heed your privately- and lovingly-expressed discipline. In such a circumstance it is important for you to realize that though there has been no mishandling of the discipline called for and consequently there is no problem within you yourself, there does remain in him—due to his failure to listen to you—the unresolved problem of his having sinned against you. Does this nonetheless mean that your responsibility has ceased? No, according to the instructions taught on this matter by the Lord Jesus, there is a further action which you, as the offended brother must initiate.

That further action calls for you to take with you one other brother, or preferably two other brethren, whose testimony can confirm every relevant fact. These other brothers and/or sisters are not to be merely your friends but are those who are respected not only by the brethren in the assembly at large but also especially by the offending brother who will thus have no cause to believe their testimony would be unfair or would be partial to you. The task of these additional brethren will be to help the offending one to recognize and acknowledge that what he had done to you was wrong.

Even so, Jesus taught that a still further step must be taken if that brother ignores what those additional brethren say but continues refusing to see his error and how it hinders the building up of the church. This further disciplinary step calls for the reporting of the matter to the entire assembly. And if he will not even listen to the church, there remains, said the Lord Jesus to His disciples, one final recourse in discipline: that "he is to be treated as though he were a Gentile pagan or a tax collector" (see Matthew 18:17b).

Just here we need to be most accurate and careful in the way we interpret or understand this statement of Jesus'. The Lord has not said that the stubborn brother is to be excommunicated, that word meaning to be cast out of, or excluded from, the church. No, this unrepentant brother has not committed the kind of sin which leads to excommunication from the assembly of God's people. An instance of *that* kind which we have in Scripture is what was supposed to happen to the particular believer in the Corinthian church who had taken his father's wife, was cohabiting with her, and had not ceased doing so when confronted with his sin. Instructed the apostle Paul when writing of this matter to the Corinthian brethren: "Cast out—expel—that wicked man from among yourselves" (see I Corinthians 5:1-2, 13b). That man and his sinning, however, is a different circumstance from the brother we are considering here who has sinned against you. This latter person has not yet committed the kind of evil which, if one is unrepentant, would lead to expulsion from the assembly of the saints.

Instead, what is to happen to this brother of yours who remains unrepentant even after refusing to heed the church's counsel and rebuke? Be it carefully understood that he is not to be cast out or expelled but is allowed to continue meeting with you and the other saints in the assembly; even so, because his fellowship with you and the other church members has been interrupted, he is to be looked upon and treated as though he were one of the defrauding tax collectors of that day or as though he were an unbelieving Gentile sinner or pagan. Nevertheless, you and the others in the church should pity him but not hate him, just as you are not to hate an unbelieving sinner in the world but would show pity towards such a person.

What has therefore just been described in some detail is how the first kind or stage of discipline—that pertaining to brotherly relationships—is to be carried out, step by step, in the church. Permit me to say, however, that if more discipline at this brotherly-relationship level or stage were exercised among church brethren today, it is my belief that there would be less need for the entire church herself to be involved in exercising the necessary discipline.

The challenge facing the church today is that we as members one of another need to rise up and discipline each other whenever it becomes necessary. We heretofore have thought that not to do so is a virtue, when actually it has been a pervasive weakness. Sad to say, we have failed to realize that we have a responsibility to discipline one another so as to build up one another, we not having discerned that by so doing we would be assisting in building up the church, the house of God. Let us see that when such brotherly- and/or sisterly-discipline is carried out among us in a right spirit and is received in equally a right spirit, such will bring us closer together. Indeed, if implemented by you in a right spirit and received by the offending brother or sister in the right spirit, this will bring you and that one even closer than before, because there is now much love evident there. Regrettably, the exercise of such spiritual discipline we have dared not do, and one of the reasons is that there has been a lack of sufficient love present among us.

Frankly, we do not love our brothers and sisters to the extent required for us to be willing to go through the oftentimes painful process necessary in restoring our brother or our sister. How needful for us to ask our Father-God to fill our hearts with sufficient love and compassion for our brethren—yet not for the purpose of seeing much better the mote in the eye of our erring brother or sister when in fact we are unable to detect the beam in our own eye. Not so! Let us instead be challenged to see that if we have been disciplined by our Father and seek to have our hearts filled with His love for our erring brethren, we shall be spiritually enabled to discipline them by helping them to at last see the mote in their eye and thus be used by the Lord to restore them to spiritual well-being. If such discipline is not occurring as it should be in the church, I am concerned that she shall always be weak in her relationships, it resulting in the lack of a real cementing together of her members.

May this first stage of discipline at the level of brotherly-relationships be fully restored to God's house, is my fervent prayer during these days.

Now there is also a second kind of discipline, and I would like for us to call it the fatherly-care type of discipline. And in this regard, I would like to place before us for our consideration two passages of Scripture:

I John 2: "I write unto you, little children, … I write unto you, fathers, … I write unto you, young men …" (vv. 12a, 13a-b; and repeated in vv. 13c, 14).

Galatians 6: "Brethren, if [anyone] be taken [or, caught] in some fault, ye who are spiritual restore such a one in a spirit of meekness [or, gentleness], considering thyself lest thou also be tempted" (v. 1). From the first passage we are given to understand that in the house of God there are members of His household who are at various stages of spiritual growth and maturity. Hence, some of the members of the church are children, some are at the stage of spiritual young men, and still others are spiritual fathers. And from the second passage, which speaks suggestively of fathers in the church, we see, in the matter of restorative discipline to be exercised in God's house, that the relationship between or among God's people which is being brought into view here has not the same character about it which exists in the relationship between brothers which we saw presented in Matthew 18. Whereas the parties concerned in Matthew—brother to brother—will be on an equal footing in their spiritual relationship one to another, in the spiritual relationship being described in the Galatians passage, the parties involved are obviously not on an equal footing one to another, it being a relationship between one who is more mature and experienced—like that of a father—and one who is much less mature and experienced, he or she having committed a fault, sin or trespass of some sort.

In other words, the first kind of discipline earlier described today is the kind carried out on the basis of a brotherly relationship, wherein you, and the brother who has sinned against you, are both more or less equal spiritually one to the other. But in what I call the fatherly-care second type of discipline as depicted in Galatians, the two parties concerned are clearly not equal in spirituality and are therefore not on an equal spiritual standing before God nor in the eyes of one another. Moreover, those in the church who have sinned or are at fault, being carnal and not spiritual, may not even realize that they have committed a sin or fault; or they may know they have fallen into sin but are not able, being spiritually immature and inexperienced, to extricate themselves from the sin or fault and its consequences.

Therefore, those in God's family who are as fathers who carefully observe and have a caring heart are moved to reach out to those who are at fault and try to restore them in a spirit of gentleness, meekness and humility. Indeed, a truly spiritual father will not approach the erring believer in an air of superiority or of looking down upon that one in a condescending manner and proceed to rebuke, scold and criticize. No, you who are spiritually much more mature are to treat the sinful brother or sister in a spirit of humility and gentleness as would a sensitive father wishing to restore his erring son or daughter to a proper standing in the family, and doing so with a fatherly care, sympathy and concern.

Hence, that is why I have chosen to call this second kind or stage of discipline the fatherly-care type. In any local gathering of believers there will be some brethren who, being more mature spiritually, have the responsibility before God as fathers to care for the less mature who have fallen into sin and to attempt to restore them. At the same time, however, those fathers, being fallen human beings themselves, must be on guard, lest they too be tempted.

Once again today, I would observe that in the church today, there is a further lack—in this case, a lack of this fatherly-care kind of discipline being exercised. It may be due, of course, to a lack of a sufficient number of spiritual fathers who are available for carrying out this type of disciplining responsibility in God's house. Yet, if there be such ones in the church, I wonder how many of those less spiritually mature ones, who may have fallen into sin, will be restored? That can only be determined by the actions of those spiritually more mature brethren who as fathers will actually take up their responsibility to exercise the necessary discipline.

There is still one final type or stage of discipline that is needed to be exercised in the house of God; and it can simply be termed church discipline, which is usually to be implemented or carried out by a local church's eldership. The Scripture basis for this final type of discipline is to be found in Hebrews 3: "… Christ is faithful as the Son over God's house. And we are his house …" (v. 6a-b NIV).

Why is it that the church must exercise discipline? It is because Christ as a faithful son has been set over God's house; and because the Son is the Head over the house of God, therefore, it must be put in order. If, as in the case of the expressions of God's house in Crete, it should fall into disorder, Christ the faithful Son must and will exercise His Headship over the house to set it right; and the discipline which must be exercised will usually be placed in the hands of the elders to be applied—and that can be termed *church* discipline in contrast to brotherly and fatherly-care types of discipline. And thus church discipline constitutes the last resort available to the church in administering the discipline required to put things in order and/or maintain that order in God's house.

Now as an instance of this kind of disciplinary action that was present in the early church expression of God's house, we will recall that reference was made earlier today to the situation in the Corinthian church of the unrepentant brother there who had taken to himself his father's wife. And when the apostle Paul exhorted the church as a whole to exercise discipline by casting out that brother from the assembly of the saints (see again I Corinthians 5:1-2, 13b), they did so; and as a consequence of this church discipline, it can be assumed from the relevant Scripture texts that that brother was eventually restored to the life and fellowship of the church (II Corinthians 2:1-11).

There is yet another example of this last recourse to church discipline. Reference was also made earlier to Paul's instruction which he issued to Titus in chapter 3 of his epistle to him to warn all those heretical, factious brethren in the Cretan churches to cease their troublemaking conduct; and if after the second warning issued they failed to do so, the brethren in the various churches were to have nothing more to do with them (v. 10).

Such church discipline has to be applied for the sake of the sanctity and unity of the church. And the ones who are responsible to exercise the authority and discipline of the Son over God's house will usually be the elders in each local assembly. If, though, the church discipline required to put things right in God's house is not exercised, there will be continuing disorder therein, and the evil influence stemming from that disorder will begin to spread until, speaking in figurative terms here both of evil influence and of God's church, like leaven, the evil influence will leaven the entire unleavened batch of bread dough, the latter of which is what the church is in fact to be like (see again I Corinthians 5:6b-7a).

It is most unfortunate that in God's house today, instead of the exercise of one or the other of the first two kinds of discipline—the brotherly and the fatherly-care types—it seems to be the case that whenever a situation arises which calls for one or the other of those types of discipline to be applied, it more often than not will be this third type—the last recourse in discipline—which is the one to be exercised *immediately*. Some, if not all, of those who have ultimate responsibility in the church can at times be so authority-minded that they forget that they are poor sinners saved by grace, and so they are inclined to exercise discipline overly severely. It too often happens that either these responsible brethren fail to discipline when they should or else when they do exercise discipline, they conduct themselves in such a manner that it is actually they who discipline the saints and not God's Son whom they are supposed to represent—and represent accurately—when applying the discipline.

This last observation leads me to conclude our consideration together today on this subject of discipline by bringing to your attention what I believe are three kinds of spirit which we must have when exercising any type of discipline; otherwise, I would not advise anyone to assume that responsibility at all.

The first necessary spirit to have has already been mentioned, which is, that one must possess a spirit of love when exercising either brotherly, fatherly-care, or church-type discipline. We all need to pray that God would truly seal our hearts with His love before we dare exercise any type of discipline in His house.

The second kind of spirit we are to possess if we dare be used to administer God's discipline in the church is that we have the spirit of a priest—that servant of God who serves both Him and His people. We are told in the Old Testament book of Leviticus, chapter 10, that the Israelite priests were to eat the sin offering offered up to God by the people. Moses had commanded Aaron the high priest and his two priestly sons to eat the people's sin offering (a goat here) as the way by which the sins of the Israelite community would be taken away (v. 17). This priestly act back then serves as a symbolic picture for how we as members of God's royal priesthood today (I Peter 2:9a) are to conduct ourselves in performing the priestly responsibility of exercising discipline whenever required among God's people in His house.

In priestly fashion, therefore, you, though not having sinned, are so deeply burdened and concerned over the sin, fault or trespass of this brother or that sister, that you recognize before God as though *you* had been the one who had sinned. In other words, and employing Old Testament language here, you as a caring priest, eat the sin offering of that brother or sister; and thus you will pray for that one in agonizing travail on his or her behalf. Only in the spirit of that kind of priestly service can you approach an erring brother or sister with the intent of exercising the proper kind of discipline for the purpose of achieving spiritual restoration.

Let me add that if anyone who seeks to exercise discipline in the church is not functioning with the spirit of a priest as just now described, then that person should not be administering any type of church discipline. Too often those who are applying discipline towards brethren in God's house today are aloof, distant, and seemingly unconcerned, the undertaking having become legalistic—even cold and harsh—in nature. And because of that, the discipline being applied fails to have the right effect, with those brethren on the receiving end rebelling against it. On the other hand, if every time the person who would exercise discipline would approach a brother who has sinned against him with tears and in the spirit of a priest, I would venture to say that in ninety percent of such instances the offending brother will react softly and receive the discipline necessary to be restored.

Now it is that kind of spirit which is very much needed in the exercise of discipline in the church today.

And the third kind of spirit a person must have, if that one is to be effective in administering discipline in God's house, is to go in the power and energy of the Holy Spirit. You who would discipline someone in the church with your own energy and power will only crush—not to say, spiritually slay—the one on the receiving end. That is not the sort of spirit for anyone exercising discipline to have which can be validated or honored anywhere in Scripture. Declared the prophet of old, "Not by [man's] might, nor by [man's] power, but by my Spirit, saith the Lord of hosts" (see Zechariah 4:6b).

In the act of disciplining a member in God's household a person must be so attuned to God almighty that he goes forth not in his own but in the Spirit's power and energy for the purpose of engaging in discipline which can and will restore. If that is the manner with which you go forth, the discipline exercised will be effective. Moreover, if that is indeed the way you approach the erring believer in the church, that believer, should he or she nonetheless refuse to heed your discipline, shall not be resisting *you* but shall be resisting the Holy Spirit. Such, then, is the third kind of spirit the saint must arm himself or herself with if he or she is to be effective in exercising discipline in the church.

This area of church responsibility which we have been considering together today is the second essential element of four which I believe must be present if

God's house is to be built—and if I may say so, it is very essential. I must confess here that I hesitated very much to speak today on this subject; nevertheless, in looking to the Lord for guidance, I came to feel deeply that this area of responsibility is extremely lacking in the church in our day and needs to be addressed. Unfortunately, it has been so much abused in the recent past that many of God's servants have dared not touch it. And because of this circumstance, we must sadly acknowledge that the church is not being set in order as it should and the house of God is not being built. The exercise of discipline is therefore very much needed. Yet, no matter what type of discipline is in fact exercised, it must be carried out in the right way and in the right spirit.

May God help in that very regard all those who shall be involved in this highly essential element of responsibility in His church.

Our heavenly Father, we have just been considering together this subject of discipline. We tremble before Thee because who are we? Thou art God and Thou art the only one who can discipline. Oh Father, seal us with Thy love that we may learn how to move into this area of discipline rightly because we are moved by Thy love—love for our brethren, love for one another, and love for the sanctity of Thy house. We pray that we will not put ourselves into this area of church responsibility, and yet *in Christ* we do put ourselves into it. Father, we do desire to see that there is more discipline exercised in Thy house because we want Thy house to be built. We want to see Thy house set in order. We want Thee to rest in Thy house, but we must look to Thy Holy Spirit to teach us and to train us in this area so that the beauty of Thy house may be manifested. We ask in the name of our Lord Jesus. Amen.

Chapter Four

Setting God's House in Order: Sound Teaching & Good Works

Titus 2:1-15—But do thou speak the things that become sound teaching; that the elder men be sober, grave, discreet, sound in faith, in love, in patience; that the elder women in like manner be in deportment as becoming those who have to say to sacred things, not slanderers, not enslaved to much wine, teachers of what is right; that they may admonish the young women to be attached to their husbands, to be attached to their children, discreet, chaste, diligent in home work, good, subject to their own husbands, that the word of God may not be evil spoken of. The younger men in like manner exhort to be discreet: in all things affording thyself as a pattern of good works; in teaching uncorruptedness, gravity, a sound word, not to be condemned; that he who is opposed may be ashamed, having no evil thing to say about us: bondmen to be subject to their own masters, to make themselves acceptable in everything; not gainsaying; not robbing their masters, but shewing all good fidelity, that they may adorn the teaching which is of our Saviour God in all things. For the grace of God which carries with it salvation for all men has appeared, teaching us that, having denied impiety and worldly lusts, we should live soberly, and justly, and piously in the present course of things, awaiting the blessed hope and appearing of the glory of our great God and Saviour Jesus Christ; who gave himself for us, that he might redeem us from all lawlessness, and purify to himself a peculiar people, zealous for good works. These things speak, and exhort, and rebuke with all authority. Let no one despise thee.

Titus 3:4-8—But when the kindness and love to man of our Saviour God appeared, not on the principle of works which have been done in righteousness which we had done, but according to his own mercy he saved us through the washing of regeneration and renewal of the Holy Spirit, which he poured out on us richly through Jesus Christ our Saviour; that, having been justified by his grace, we should become heirs according to the hope of eternal life. The word is faithful, and I desire that thou insist strenuously on these things, that they who have believed God take care to pay diligent attention to good works. These things are good and profitable to men.

We have already considered together how God raised up the young man Titus to be a kind of troubleshooter for resolving difficult and disorderly conditions in His house. God first developed in Titus such sterling character that he was a ready vessel in the hands of his Master. And we look to Him to raise up many young men and women in our day with solid Christian character as was in Titus. I think this is the greatest need in our time; and with such people as this, God will be able to set His house in order during the period which remains in this final age of world history. Indeed, in his letter to Titus the apostle Paul is found giving his younger fellow worker instructions on how to set the house of God in order; or to describe the matter another way, the apostle gave instructions to Titus on how to build God's house to His satisfaction.

In reviewing further our previous considerations together it was pointed out that there are four elements or principles which are absolutely essential to be present and operational in the church if God's house is to be built, with spiritual leadership and spiritual discipline being the first two essentials required if any disorderly expression of the church is to be successfully set in order and if God's house is to be built to His satisfaction. And today I would like for us to look closely into the remaining two essentials: sound teaching and good works.

Sound Teaching

Paul's Titus epistle makes clear that in Crete there was an incredible lack of sound teaching, which had created serious disorderly conditions throughout the island's assemblies of God's people. This we find revealed in the epistle's very first chapter:

... there are many and disorderly vain speakers and deceivers of people's minds, specially those of the circumcision, who must have their mouths stopped, who subvert whole houses, teaching things which ought not to be taught for the sake of base gain (vv. 10-11).

The Cretan churches were confronted with a truly major problem because there were many—not just a few or some but many—disorderly people who did not subject themselves to authority or to the rule of God. There were vain speakers who were mouthing many empty words, were deceiving people's minds, and were teaching various notions and thoughts which ought not to be taught. Among them were the Judaizers—those of the circumcision party—who loved to talk about Jewish fables and the traditions and commandments of men instead of the truth of God (1:14). Therefore, with all these false teachings and false teachers in their midst—they being in great number—no wonder Paul was deeply concerned that their mouths must be stopped. They must be severely rebuked (1:13b) so that people would not any longer be led astray from the truth of God.

This was not a problem peculiar only to the churches in Crete; to the contrary, ever since the later period of ministry by Jesus' earliest apostles, and continuing thereafter throughout church history right up to the present day, this has been a serious problem in the church. In sharp contrast to that dismal fact, however, we learned in one of our previous sessions together that during the very earliest period of church history, immediately after God by His Spirit had formed His church on earth on the day of Pentecost, those who believed were together and continued in the teaching and the fellowship of the apostles and in the breaking of bread and prayers. In other words, during that earliest church period God's people were nurtured with the sound teaching of the Lord's apostles; moreover, they practiced that teaching by continuing in the fellowship of the apostles. Here, then, was simplicity and truth, and there was nothing more and better with which to build up God's people and therefore build God's house than the word of His grace (Acts 2:41-42, 44a, 46; 20:32).

The truth and significance of that last phrase—the word of His grace—was in fact emphasized by the apostle Paul on one occasion. We may recall that at the eastern Mediterranean seaport of Miletus he had from there summoned the Ephesian church elders to come to him that he might speak to them some parting words of counsel (Acts 20:17-18a). And among his concluding words to those elders were these: "And now, brethren, I commit you to God and to the word of His grace, which is able to build you up and give to you an inheritance among all His consecrated people" (see again v. 32).

In so many words Paul was here affirming the truth that sound teaching is that which builds up the church. We may also state the obverse of that assertion and still be correct: Nothing tears down the church more easily or more quickly than unsound, false teaching. And in Crete, because there were many false teachers speaking forth an immense amount of unsound—even false—teaching, the result was division among God's people. That is why in his epistle to Titus Paul had to issue to his co-worker the severe instruction concerning all those so-called brethren in the Cretan churches whom the apostle described as "heretical" or "factious" (3:10a Darby, NASB). As was pointed out during our last time together, these were men who were widely disseminating throughout the island's assemblies a confusing mixture of opinions and false notions which were causing division among the believers along the lines of this or that school of opinion or thought. Such factious, divisive, heretical subversives in the churches, declared Paul, must be admonished to cease their propagandizing activity by issuing a first and a second warning; and if not heeded, then "reject" them by having "nothing [more] to do with them" (v. 10b NASB, NIV). These churches were confronted with a truly serious problem.

Throughout most of church history there has been the same problem which has confronted the true churches of God. One could date the beginning of this unfortunate circumstance from the days of the ministry of Barnabas and Paul in, and out elsewhere from, the Syrian church of Antioch. It will be remembered from Acts 15 that certain Judaizing believers in Christ had come down from Jerusalem to Antioch and had begun teaching in the church there a confusing so-called gospel message which asserted that Gentile believers not only must have accepted Christ but they also must undergo circumcision and observe the rest of the Mosaic Law if they were to be perfect in their faith. And we will recall that those two apostles were commissioned by the mostly Gentile saints in the Antiochan church to travel up to Jerusalem for the settling of this issue. And though it *was* settled in Jerusalem, it was not really settled in many places elsewhere because those Jerusalem Judaizers commenced following Paul wherever he went. This development constituted a never-ending headache for this apostle and for some of the other earliest apostles of Jesus, as is reflected in the epistles written by them in later years: those such as Galatians, II Timothy, II Peter, I John, and Jude.

It cannot be denied that back then there was an ever-ongoing problem for the true churches of that day to have to contend with: the continuing presence and activity of numerous false teachers, prophets, and even apostles. Not only was there the Jewish influence in attempting to Judaize the Christian faith by mixing up Law with grace (the Galatians epistle, Titus 1:10a) and the spreading of false teachings surrounding Jewish traditions and commandments of men and Jewish fables and myths (Titus 1:10b, 14a); there were, as well, the worthless and unprofitable teachings and so-called philosophies of nascent Gnosticism (cf. Titus 3:9) which had gradually commenced invading the churches in subsequent days.

In fact, except for the earliest period of church history in Jerusalem, Judea, Samaria, Galilee,

Damascus, and a few other places, the true church of God has never really been free from the influence of false teachings. And in our own day, the churches are in no better state in relation to such false influence than in those earlier days, and perhaps today's church may be in even a worse condition. For not only are there false teachings present in various religious cults, some of them pretending to be Christian in character; even in certain evangelical churches can be found some teachings being disseminated that are actually not based upon God's word at all. False teaching poses a very serious challenge for the church today if the building of the house of God is to be achieved.

How, then, are these false teachers and their teachings which tear down and even destroy the church of Christ to be combated? As we have come to see, on the one hand, in each assembly discipline needs to be present and functioning: stop the mouths of those vain talkers in the midst (1:11a), rebuke them sharply (1:13b), and, if need be after admonishing them once and twice with warnings, be done with them totally if they refuse to heed those disciplinary warnings (3:10b), thus purifying the church entirely from their deteriorating influence.

Yet that is only the negative side in combating false teaching. The best way to combat it, and which forms the positive side in the matter, is to have sound teaching coming forth in the assembly of the believers.

A careful reading of the Titus epistle will yield the fact that this very word sound is repeated numerous times throughout its text. Indeed, at the very beginning of the letter Paul's introductory words set forth an intimation of sound teaching: "Paul, servant of God and apostle of Jesus Christ—sent to help God's chosen people to believe and know the truth which promotes godliness" (1:1 Beck). Is that not sound teaching? Also, in the opening chapter's verse 9 the apostle includes among the qualifications of an acceptable church leader this one: "... that he can encourage others by sound doctrine and refute those who oppose it" (NIV).

Further, Paul writes in chapter 2 the following advice to Titus: "... speak the things which are fitting for sound teaching" (see v.1). And Paul gives additional advice to Titus on what his teaching should be like: "Do not let anything corrupt your teaching; be grave and serious in your teaching; and let your teaching be sound and wholesome so that it will be beyond reproach" (see 2:7-8a). Even the older women are exhorted to be teachers of "what is right and good" (see 2:3c Amplified).

Here the apostle states that what is to be taught is the pure word of God which has not been corrupted by there having been mixed in with it such things as fables, myths, commandments of man's creation, empty talk, speculations and arguments of all kinds or any other Gnostic notion. Moreover, the way to preach sound teaching is for the teacher to be serious and weighty in his manner and not lighthearted. Furthermore, the very speech employed is to be couched in sound and wholesome words. Oh, how the church is in need of sound, wholesome and healthy teaching which can be instrumental in building the house of God!

Now with regard to this subject of sound teaching, two examples of it have been provided for us in this very epistle of Paul's to Titus—the first is in 2:11-14 and the second, in 3:5-7. Their words can be found embedded within the two quoted texts from Titus which serve as the introduction to our time in God's word together today on the two essential elements of sound teaching and good works. It is my hope and prayer today that by our reviewing these two examples we shall be able to recognize the kind of teaching which is sound and which can be used to build up the church.

Let us take up the first example from Titus chapter 2. We are told in verses 11 and 13 of two appearances separated in time: one of which has occurred already and the other one we are looking forward to its being fulfilled. Thus, firstly, the grace of God which brings salvation for all men has already appeared; and, secondly, what we are looking and waiting for is the blessed hope of the appearing of the glory of our great God and Savior Jesus Christ. The content of both these appearances spoken of in God's word—the grace of God and the blessed hope—constitute sound teaching. And when correctly taught in some detail they together form an extensive example of sound teaching which cannot be condemned and is beyond reproach. Therefore, with the Holy Spirit's help this extensive example of sound teaching is what I would now like to place before us for our consideration.

When the grace of God appeared, it brought with it salvation for all men. That is the grace of God, the fact that we are saved through the Lord Jesus Christ, just as Paul has written elsewhere in God's word: "You are saved by grace through faith in Christ, and this is not of yourself; it is God's gift" (see Ephesians 2:8); and that is an element of sound teaching.

That, however, is merely the beginning, for the Titus 2 passage continues by saying, "teaching us." That word teaching in the original Greek conveys the thought of training, disciplining, instructing, educating. So what does the grace of God do to us? Yes, it brings salvation to us in that we are saved by grace, but is that all? Unfortunately, in much false teaching the emphasis is not on the grace of God but is placed on the work of man. Even in much of what we would term correct teaching, all we hear being stressed is the grace of God that has brought salvation to all men, and that is the extent of what is understood and taught to be the meaning and content of God's grace. Most certainly we must thank God that we are saved; but is that all? According to such teaching it would seem to be the case that after a person is saved, there is nothing more for that one to do except wait for death and then enter into eternal life.

However, let it be clearly understood that *sound* teaching on the grace of God includes not only the setting forth of the fact that His grace *saved* us (past effect) but includes also the setting forth of the fact that His grace *in the present* is continually training, instructing, teaching and disciplining us. For what purpose? The Titus 2 passage again does not leave us in the dark but informs us what the purpose of God's grace is for doing in our present lives; for its further words read like this in the NASB translation: "instructing us to deny ungodliness and worldly desires and to live sensibly, righteously and godly in the present age" (v. 12).

Upon our having received the grace of God in initially saving us through Christ Jesus, this grace will commence its present saving work in us by means of child-training and disciplining us. This grace will discipline us in such a way that we are being delivered from impiety and worldly lusts. It is not enough for us to be saved from our past sins by having our past sins forgiven; no, God's grace does a further work in the present for us, which is, to deliver us from all forms of ungodliness. Whatever is not like God in your daily life is that which is ungodly; and so, God by His wondrous grace will deliver you from such ungodliness and worldly lusts—the lust of the flesh, the lust of the eyes and the pride of life (I John 2:16).

What a present deliverance we need to experience through the grace of God! His grace not only has provided for us in the past but it also is providing for us in the present. His grace is sufficient for these present days in our Christian walk.

Negatively speaking, we are delivered by God's grace from anything which is not like Him, anything which smells of the world, of the flesh, of ourselves. Then, speaking positively, His grace brings us into a life that lives sensibly or soberly. The Greek word translated as soberly in English has the thought of possessing a sound mind, which calls to mind the traits of discipline, order, restraint, having control, being mentally healthy. With respect to ourselves, we are to live a sober, healthy, well-balanced, well-ordered, well-disciplined kind of life. With respect to our relationship with people in the world, we are to be just; for example, in our relationship with unbelieving neighbors, we are to be just, fair, and honest—thus bearing a good testimony. And with respect to our life with God, we are to live in a godly manner in all things. That, then, is what the grace of God can do for us in exerting both a necessary negative and necessary positive effect upon us during this present time of ours on the earth.

Furthermore, the grace of God can and should also have an effect upon us for the future, in that it prepares us for the future: "… awaiting the blessed hope and appearing of the glory of our great God and Saviour Jesus Christ." We are waiting for the glory of God, our Lord Jesus Christ, to appear so that we can stand before Him unashamed (cf. I John 2:28).

Finally, this Titus 2 passage, exemplifying as it does sound teaching, concludes with this noble thought: "… Christ …, who gave himself for us." This is what the Lord Jesus has done for us. But unto what purpose? "… that he might redeem us from all lawlessness, and purify to himself a peculiar people, zealous for good works." Jesus has redeemed us at such a costly price in having delivered us fallen sinners from all lawlessness so that He might purify for himself a special people for His own possession and who shall be zealous to do good works. And hence, we have come to see that the grace of God touches in an immensely beneficial way upon believers' past, their present, and their future.

In summing up on this Titus 2 passage as an excellent example of sound teaching, I would need to add here that any teaching which is in line with what has been presented in some detail concerning the grace of God is indeed sound. On the other hand, the lack of any aspect of that which has been expressed here regarding what Paul has written in this Titus 2 passage and what has been presented from other verses in God's word related to the grace of God is teaching which is unbalanced, imperfect and incomplete. Moreover, it can humbly be said that the kind of sound teaching as just now delineated in some detail during the past few minutes ought, when taught, to have a healthy, wholesome effect upon believers' lives in their present day-to-day walk before the Lord. And further, such sound teaching, if properly taught in the church, cannot but assist greatly in countering, any and all disorderly elements which may be present in the church, and cannot but also result in the building of God's house.

Oh, may we look to God that He will raise up many teachers who are able to teach in such a healthy, sound manner that it shall result in a healthy church.

The second passage—the one in Titus 3—is another specimen, and a very good one, of what sound teaching is. Paul wrote in verse 4: "… when the kindness and love to man of our Savior God appeared." This kindness and love have their origin in God and nowhere else. What is kindness? It is the practical expression of goodness. God is good (Mark 10:18b), and out of His goodness comes forth kindness towards us. The phrase, "the … love towards man" in the Greek original happens to be the source for our English word philanthropy (*phileo* = love, *anthropos* = man). And it is well known that a philanthropist is one who is highly generous and very liberal in giving of his substance towards the poor and needy of every sort. We may therefore say that the extremely generous liberality of God's kindness has indeed appeared to us.

Let us notice that this description of Paul's is in contrast to the words of his in verse 3 which speaks of our having been "hateful, and hating one another." On God's part there is abundant kindness and love which is in great contrast to what we were: only hatred and meanness on our part. And this kindness—this plentiful liberality—on the part of our Savior God appeared for the purpose of saving us, adds the apostle; yet He saved us not on the basis of any works in presumed righteousness of ours; nor was it because of our having gained any merit—we actually have none—but His saving of us was purely according to His mercy. This the apostle made clear in verse 5.

By what means, though, did God save us? We are told in the rest of verse 5 and verse 6 that He saved us "by the washing of regeneration and renewal of the Holy Spirit, which He poured out on us richly through Jesus Christ our Saviour."

Just here I must interject a brief explanation concerning the phrase, the washing of regeneration. This is because some Christians have interpreted this phrase as signifying baptismal regeneration, the meaning of which is that regeneration—or, the new birth—occurs in a person through or as a result of experiencing the act of water baptism. We must look into this matter carefully, since our purpose in considering together this Titus 3 passage is to discern how it is an example of good sound teaching.

We realize, of course, that this English word regeneration, translated from the Greek original, means "new birth." Interestingly, this word is only found twice in the entire New Testament—once here in Titus and the other time in Matthew 19:28, which reads: "And Jesus said to them, Verily I say unto you, That ye who have followed me, in the regeneration when the Son of man shall sit down upon his throne of glory, ye also shall sit on twelve thrones, judging the twelve tribes of Israel." It is clear that in this latter passage the use of the word regeneration does not refer to an individual person's born-again or new-birth experience but refers to a regeneration of this entire world.

One future day this world shall enter upon a new phase: it shall be regenerated and brought into a new position or condition or state because Christ as the King of kings shall be on the throne with righteousness ruling over the earth (Psalm 96:13; Isaiah 32:1; Jeremiah 23:5; Revelation 19:15-16, 20:4; II Peter 3:13; Revelation 21:1-7), which is a condition obviously not at all currently true of it. Hence, the regeneration in view here is that of the world: a new age will be ushered into existence, in which there shall be a transfer or complete change from the old state of the world in *un*righteousness to a new and righteous state or position—a new birth of the world, as it were.

Having thus explained this word's use in Matthew, we come now to the use of this same word of regeneration as it appears in Titus 3. Most Bible scholars and commentators agree that this word in the Titus context, if it does not refer *directly* to water baptism, it nonetheless does have something to do with it. And because of this agreement surrounding the word as used here, some interpreters of this Titus passage believe that what is meant by its use is *baptismal* regeneration: that by means of the water in baptism by immersion a person experiences the spiritual new birth. However, we know from other Scriptures that this cannot be the teaching here; rather, what is in view by the use of the word regeneration here, as is the case in Matthew 19, is a change in position for and by the believer.

What, then, does water baptism do to, or for, us believers? For, again, we know from other Scriptures that water does not and cannot wash away our sins; only the precious blood of Christ can do that. Hence, there must be a different and correct interpretation of the phrase, the washing of regeneration, as used here in Titus than that it refers to baptismal regeneration. And if that be the case, then this phrase, joining together as it does the words washing and regeneration, must instead refer, indeed, to the act of water baptism but signifying *not* the inward experience of believers' new birth in Christ for the remission of sins but signifying the inward experience—the inward reality—of having received a new position in Christ. They no longer belong to the world but have been delivered out of that dark kingdom ruled by the Prince of Darkness (cf. Luke 22:53; Colossians 1:13a) and been translated or transferred into the kingdom of the Son of God's love (Colossians 1:13b). That is the meaning of Paul's statement that God "saved us through the washing of regeneration," it having established in believers their new position in Christ Jesus. And this inward experience of having received this new position in Him is sealed or confirmed by undergoing the outward act of water baptism.

A portion of Acts chapter 2's text can perhaps help us to understand this matter better. In the apostle Peter's inaugural gospel sermon on the day of Pentecost delivered before the Jerusalem populace of that day, he declared in part the following: "Repent, and be baptized every one of you in the name of Jesus Christ ..., and ye shall receive the gift of the Holy Spirit. ... Be saved from this perverse generation [or, from this crooked age]!" (vv. 38, 40b) Here we have before us the same two elements for being *in this particular sense* saved by God which are mentioned in the Titus 3 passage: water baptism and the gift and work of the Holy Spirit.

Concerning the first of these two elements, we are given to see by these words of Christ's apostle that having experienced the new birth through repentance and faith in Christ these new believers were saved from the perverse and crooked age or generation to which they had previously belonged. Having now been delivered out of that corrupt age and thus separated from their old relationships therein, these believers entered upon a new position in Christ, the inward reality of which was sealed or confirmed as having definitely occurred by their having undergone the outward act of water baptism.

We must next turn to the second element by which God saved those new believers on the day of Pentecost: they received the promised gift of the Holy Spirit upon their repentance and belief in Christ. This element is more fully explained by the apostle Paul in the Titus 3 passage. There he declared this: that God "saved us through the … renewal of the Holy Spirit, which he poured out on us richly through Jesus Christ our Saviour" (vv. 5a, 6 Darby). A more accurate translation of this portion of the Titus passage can be found in the NASB version of the New Testament: that God "saved us … by the … renewing by the Holy Spirit, whom He poured out upon us richly through Jesus Christ our Savior."

Here we are given to see that in contrast to the first element's "washing of regeneration" which is a once-for-all act in God having granted us believers a new position in Christ, the "renewing by the Holy Spirit" speaks of the ongoing action or work of sanctification in us believers. After God has changed our position from out of Adam into Christ, the Holy Spirit then commences His day-by-day ongoing work of renewing in our life until we be transformed and fully conformed to the image of Christ (Romans 12:2, 8:29a). Hence, this latter element is a continuing process.

However, in order for the Holy Spirit to renew us fully we need to yield ourselves in obedience to Him on a daily basis. Whereas the washing of regeneration is a once-for-all step of faith, the renewing work of the Spirit in our lives as believers requires the continuous action of obedience. Thus both elements by which God saves us bring us, respectively, into a new position of henceforth being in Christ and out of Adam and into a new life in the Spirit who, Paul further tells us in Titus 3, has been poured out upon us richly—abundantly—through Christ, even as happened to those new believers on the day of Pentecost. And now, "having been justified by [God's] grace," we "should become heirs according to the hope of eternal life" (3:7).

All this which has just now been shared during the last few minutes constitute, may I once again humbly say, the kind of sound teaching which should foster in those needy Cretan believers a holy desire to live a life in the Spirit that is worthy of their becoming heirs of eternal life. Sound teaching such as this will build up the church and at the same time can serve as a rebuke to the gainsayers who would deny the truth of the gospel of Christ. Moreover, sound teaching of this kind, if "stressed" often enough (3:8a NIV), shall have the effect, as Paul declared, of causing the Cretan saints to be careful "to pay diligent attention to [doing] good works" (3:8b Darby).

May God truly raise up among His people everywhere in our day those who can bring forth sound teaching which can assist greatly in the building of His house. Oh, how sound teaching is vitally needed in God's church today!

Good Works

Now as we have just learned from Paul's words in Titus 3:8, there is a natural, logical connection between sound teaching and good works. This truth can be further borne out by stating the opposite connection: false or *un*sound teaching will corrupt our conduct, resulting in bad or unprofitable or worthless works. Titus chapter 1 informs us of this very result: "… that they may be sound in the faith, not turning their minds to Jewish fables and commandments of men, turning away from the truth. All things are pure to the pure; but to the defiled and unbelieving nothing is pure; but both their mind and their conscience are defiled" (vv. 14-15).

Here we are told that false or unsound teaching will result in the defiling of the mind and the conscience. False teaching defiles our mind in leading it away from the truth as it is in Christ, it becoming a distorted, even a reprobate, mind; and that negative development in turn affects our conscience in a negative way. In other words, not only the mind of a person who is carried away from the truth by false teaching becomes muddled and defiled, but that person's conscience likewise becomes muddled and defiled: it is no longer sensitive to the voice of the Holy Spirit.

That very circumstance explains a great deal to those of us who may wonder how it is that people who profess to be Christians can do certain ungodly things without their consciences bothering them at all. The explanation lies just here: it is because various false teachings have already defiled both their minds and consciences to such an extent that even though, as the next verse indicates, such people "profess to know God," their very "works deny him," they having become "abominable."

Interestingly enough, in the Greek original, the word translated into English as abominable appears only once in the entire New Testament, and it is found here in this Titus verse 16. What does it mean? In one word, in God's eyes, the people being spoken about here are *detestable*. Now morally and completely corrupted and perverted in their conduct, such people—though they have openly claimed to know God—deny Him by their deeds, they having become, as verse 16 intimates, disobedient to His word and become worthless for any good work.

We need, of course, to define what good works are. First of all, I believe we all realize that we are not saved by any good works of ours. Before our having known the Lord Jesus as Savior, most likely all of us thought that we could be saved by performing good works. Such has been the case from the very inception of human history. For instance, after Adam and Eve had eaten the forbidden fruit, immediately they sought to cover their nakedness by weaving fig leaves together into aprons and placing them upon themselves—an obvious example of a good work (Genesis 3:7). Then, too, Cain had offered up to God, as the result of his labor, the first fruit of the produce of his fields, he thinking that this should certainly appease God's wrath—another example of a good work (Genesis 4:3).

How we humans have continually relied upon good works for our salvation ever since, we incorrectly assuming that by so doing we gain for ourselves merits from our good works which will thus satisfy a righteous God. Our assumption has always been that there is worth and merit to be derived from performing good works of all kinds which could then be offered up as that which could and would appease the anger of God. And such an assumption has served as the fundamental basis underpinning the thought and practice of all religions.

But we can thank God that at a certain point in our lives we were given to see and understand that all our assumed righteousnesses were and are as filthy rags in God's sight (Isaiah 64:6a). We ultimately realized that we cannot depend on our so-called righteous merits supposedly derived from our good works for our personal salvation; instead, we came to see that we could only depend on the righteous merits of the Lord Jesus in order to be saved.

However, we can go to the other extreme by not doing any good works after being saved, which is not true according to God's word. Yes, indeed, we are *not saved* by good works, but according to the word of God we are saved *to do* good works. After being saved we are supposed to do good works as God's word says in Ephesians chapter 2: "we are His workmanship, having been created in Christ Jesus for good works, which God prepared beforehand that we should walk in them" (v. 10 NKJV).

From this and other Scriptures we are given to understand that there is a definite place for good works. Good works please God, and if you have done good works, you will be rewarded by Him.

Before proceeding further, however, I believe it is important for us to know what good works are. Usually we think of good works as doing those which are good in the eyes of man. Strictly speaking, however, that is not true. Only God is good (Mark 10:18b), therefore, good works are works which are done according to the will of God: good works are those which are done by His power and done for His glory: only such as these are good works. We are a special people of His who are to do good works as just now defined. In other words, we are saved to do the will of God, whatever that will may be.

Now sometimes the will of God may not appear good in your eyes or mine, or it may not seem good in the eyes of the world; but such are good works because they are done in accordance with the will of God. Not only are they done according to His will, they are also done in His power, and for His glory.

Towards the end of the so-called Sermon on the Mount the Lord is heard saying the following: "Not all who call Me Lord, Lord shall enter the kingdom. True, many will come to Me and say, 'Lord, we have done this for You in Your name: we have cast out demons, healed the sick, and preached the gospel— we have done all such works for You and in Your name.' But I will say to them, 'Depart from me, workers of lawlessness; I do not know you'" (see Matthew 7:21-23). Will they not have been doing good works? Yet the Lord shall declare to them: "You are wicked; I do not approve of you or your works." Why will that be His reaction? Simply because they shall have been doing such works according to their own desire, in their own power and for their own glory. Therefore, we who are saved should be taught correctly how to do good works, they being nothing but those works undertaken according to the will of God. When Jesus was upon earth, He traveled around doing good, they being good works because they were all the will of God.

Now the letter of the apostle Paul's to Titus is full of suggested good works which believers ought to do. And though this letter has been arbitrarily divided into three chapters, they each can be viewed as containing good works in one of three different areas of our lives as Christians. Accordingly, it can be observed that chapter 1 includes the mention of one or more good works in our church life; chapter 2, one or more good works in our family life; and chapter 3, one or more in our social life. Hence, it could justifiably be said that through sound teaching there can be the recognition of the fact that there are good works in every area of our lives.

What, then, are the good works which can be found in chapter 1 having to do with church life? There it mentions elders; and in his epistle of I Timothy, the apostle states that whoever aspires to be an overseer (or elder) in the church, is actually aspiring to do "a good work" (3:1). Let it be clearly understood here that it is not a matter of someone being ambitious to acquire a good position in the church but that the person is desirous of doing a good work.

Why is it that to be an overseer or elder is considered by Paul to be a good work? It is a good work because if you faithfully carry out this responsibility, you are being used by God to build up His church, which is what He wants and greatly desires. In other words, it is a good work because it is fulfilling His will.

If, of course, you wish to be clever and not desire to become an overseer, you are free to do so; and thus you can murmur, complain, and criticize the person who does aspire to do this good work and becomes this kind of responsible church leader; whereas if you become an overseer yourself, then you will be the one who shall be criticized and murmured against.

It needs to be emphasized that a true overseer is not one who positions himself above and issues orders and who is then served by everybody else. Not so. An overseer, according to the Scriptures, is one who humbly positions himself, as it were, underneath the rest of the brethren in the church and tries to support and give supply. And in the process of his providing leadership in this humble manner, he will be stepped on, murmured about, and often misunderstood.

It is often the case among church brethren that there are those who deliberately shun responsibility because they dislike having to bear responsibility of almost any sort. Indeed, they would rather let other brothers and sisters do so, because then they are free—not only because they are therefore free of any church burdens themselves but also because they are free to criticize those who do bear those burdens of responsibility: if the latter do well in leading the church, the freedom-loving brethren reap and enjoy the benefits; but if the responsible ones do not do well or make some mistakes, the freedom-loving believers have the privilege to criticize and complain. Regrettably today, too many saints are too clever for their own spiritual good and that of the church, and do not aspire to undertake any good works in their church life.

Sound teaching should produce people with the desire to do good works. In other words, if we are taught rightly in the church, we will come to acknowledge that every brother and sister has a responsibility in the building of God's house, that responsibility is what is common to every member of the body of Christ. Yet sound teaching will make it clear that with regard to bearing responsibility, there are differences in degree in doing so, and that there are differences in areas of responsibility and who should be the ones to bear responsibility in those different areas. Nevertheless, sound teaching in the church will also make clear to the saints that the concept is terribly wrong which posits the notion that only some brothers or sisters have responsibility in God's house while others do not.

The lack of the kind of sound teaching which refutes that terribly wrong notion poses a very serious problem in the church today. For in many places where God's people meet, there are those Christians who entertain this faulty concept in their thinking; namely, that the church belongs to the leaders and those leaders are expected to work themselves to death while the rest of the members in the church bear no responsibility whatsoever.

Sound teaching must be that which reminds the saints that all of the brethren in the church are God's peculiar—that is, God's special—people who, having been saved, are His workmanship, and are created in Christ Jesus for doing good works which God had planned beforehand for them to do (Ephesians 2:10 NASB, Williams). And thus, sound teaching must further stress the truth that taking up responsibility before God in His house is a good work and one which they must aspire to do. An unhealthy, unsound teaching is one which allows responsibility to fall into the hands of only one or a few, while letting the rest of God's saints be lazy lay people. Church teaching which is truly sound, however, will stir brethren to see that all members in God's house are to take up responsibility in doing good works of all kinds, and should especially produce those who will aspire to oversee: such ones will desire after good works because they want to serve.

Now just as there is a natural connection between sound teaching and good works, there is likewise a connection between good works and the exercise of discipline. It is understandable, of course, that, generally speaking, it can be said that nobody wishes to do the good work of disciplining those in the church who need correction of one sort or another. It is not only the case that no one wishes to *receive* discipline, no one also wishes to dish it out upon others; for in doing the latter we make ourselves highly unpopular. We would much rather be looked upon as nice, sweet, lovable; in short, we want to be popular among our fellow brethren.

On the one hand, there is something kindly and commendable to be said about those who do not wish to discipline others; indeed, there should never be the obsessive urge to want to discipline others as some people in fact have; that is a wrong aspiration to have. On the other hand, we may go to the opposite extreme of not wanting ever to exercise any discipline in God's house where it is obviously necessary. Because we do not discipline *ourselves*, we therefore do not wish to discipline others. In truth, that is escaping the doing of one very important good work in the church: the needful discipline of one's fellow brethren. Good works include the exercise of discipline because through discipline, saints grow and mature in their spiritual life; through discipline, order out of any disorder in the church is restored; and through discipline, God's house is that much further built to His satisfaction.

There is also a connection between good works and the functioning by all the members of Christ's body according to the grace and gift which God has granted to each one (Romans 12:5ff.). What He has given to each one of us—whether it be described in Scripture as a talent, mina, gift, or grace—is not to be buried. To the contrary, it is supposed to be traded or worked with; in fact, it serves as our working capital, so to speak (Matthew 25:14ff.). Regardless if it be one talent, two talents, or five talents, the essential thing is that the talent or talents be used for the building up of the church and not lie unutilized (Matthew 25:18, 24-28).

The problem is that the two- and five-talent brethren tend to be overworked whereas the one-talent saints tend to not work at all! The solution is for sound teaching to come forth which stresses the truth from God's word that every talent in the church must, as it were, be put into circulation (Matthew 25:27); and that by so doing, the reality of every member functioning—according to his or her talent, gift or grace—shall bring richness to the church. And that is a good work.

It bears to be repeated here that we believers, having been saved by grace and not by works, are nonetheless created in Christ Jesus for the purpose of doing good works—the very works which beforehand God had planned and prepared for us to do (Ephesians 2:10). And hence, every brother and sister must function in the house of God by doing the good work or works which have been foreordained for them to perform. Teaching in the church which puts forth all the aforementioned truths before the saints is sound teaching, indeed, and shall produce good works in abundance in God's church.

Titus chapter 2 in part is full of teaching having to do with the conduct and behavior of each adult member of all the Cretan church's many families, including that of the slaves in relation to their masters. Apparently, the apostle Paul had found it vitally necessary to provide his younger fellow worker with so much teaching in the area of family life and family relationships. For let us not forget the assessment of the Cretan national character—confirmed by Paul himself as having been true testimony—which one of their own Cretan countrymen, a prophet, had testified: namely, that "the Cretans as a whole are always liars, were like uncontrollable wild animals, and were lazy and gluttonous." And hence, for Cretans—even Christians among them—to be changed from such bad character to good Christian character would require the application by the power of the Holy Spirit of much sound teaching upon each adult family member.

We therefore find that the substance of Paul's teaching which Titus is to make known is wholesome, fitting, sound, potentially very productive of good works, and quite complete. In view throughout this chapter are the intended good works which are to come forth from the church's elderly men, elderly women, young women, young men, as well as from slaves in their relations with their masters. Such sound teaching as is reflected in this chapter should indeed produce all kinds of good works within the family setting. For example, older men are to be temperate, dignified, sensible, sound in faith, love and persever-ance (see v. 2 NASB).

Likewise, the elderly women in their deportment are to be reverent in all things as holy women. Some years ago an older sister in the Lord complained, "For us sisters, there is nothing to do but be in the kitchen." That is not true; there are many good works which they can undertake and accomplish. Not only are they to be holy and reverent in their behavior, they are also to be teachers of what is right. Moreover, they are to admonish—that is, train and instruct—the young women in the church to love both their husbands and their children, to be pure, diligent in their work at home, good, and be subject to their husbands. Hence, there are many good works for the older women in the church to do. In fact, the reason there needs to be these good works done by these women is for the sake of God's word, that it might not be dishonored, slandered or spoken evilly against in reproach (v. 5, various Bible versions). Let us be mindful, furthermore, that all these good works shall be the result of sound teaching to be taught on the part of those in the church like a Titus and the sound teaching to be given on the part of the older church women who, by their very life, can set a worthy example for the young women in the church to follow.

Then, too, those in the church who are slaves are to be taught to be subject to their masters in all things, to be well-pleasing and not argumentative, are not to steal from them, and are to be faithful in all their service; in order that all which they do may adorn, or show the beauty of, the teaching of the Savior God (vv. 9-10, various Bible versions).

Furthermore, by what was observed earlier, not only have we come to realize that sound teaching and good works must operate in tandem in relation to the church's older men and women as well as to the young women and the slaves; the same must be true with respect to the church's young men. Paul, in fact, told Titus to urge them to be sensible by using good judgment; and since Titus himself was a young man, the apostle instructed him to set an example for the church's young men by doing various good works himself, and by being sincere, serious and sound in his teaching, that if so, will be beyond reproach, and thus will shut the mouths of all opponents.

In brief, therefore, the primary import of Titus chapter 2 is simply this: every member in the family setting is to be governed in his or her deportment by sound teaching; and if the teaching is in fact sound, it should produce many good works. And the outcome will be that all the members as well as the slaves in all the families in the church will be enabled to assume and maintain their proper role and place, conduct themselves in a healthy manner, and carry out their family responsibilities well. And if such an all-embracing outcome is realized, what a testimony that must surely be to the rest of the Cretans on the island!

The initial three verses of Titus chapter 3 are devoted to the area of the Cretan Christians' social life in relation to the world in terms of their obligations to be obedient to the secular rulers and to conduct themselves peaceably, harmlessly and inoffensively towards those in the general society. Those Cretan believers who would receive sound teaching along the line of the first obligation would, if obedient to that teaching, voluntarily submit themselves to the authority of those in the world who rule. It was very important for the apostle to instruct Titus to remind church members about this matter. This was because, as was learned in chapter 1 of Titus, back then the Cretans in general were naturally quite rebellious and disobedient (vv. 10, 16). Especially was this true of the many Jews who had settled on the island, particularly the Zealots of the circumcision party (v. 10b), who never recognized the secular authority of Rome. Hence, Paul wrote for Titus to remind brethren in the church to be sure to submit themselves to the ones in the world whom God had placed over them and to be obedient. Such teaching, of course, is in line with what this same apostle had taught in chapter 13 of his Romans epistle (vv. 1-7).

With regard to the Cretan believers' second social obligation, Paul further instructed Titus to remind all the saints in the Cretan churches not to speak evil of anyone, not to be contentious but to be gentle and considerate towards all people in or outside the church, and to be ready to do every kind of good work. In other words, the Cretan believers were to bear a good testimony before the watching world.

This very conduct we, too, must manifest in our day. Let us be mindful, however, that these various good works carried out towards those in the general society are not to be the result of our own efforts in cultivating and improving our natural self-life or in beautifying our flesh. To the contrary, such good works are to be the result of the grace of God in our lives. For just as was to be the case in the lives of the believers in the Cretan church, upon ourselves receiving sound teaching, the grace of God would, by means of the Holy Spirit, begin to work in us to produce good character in us—even the character of Christ. And if that be true of us, then all our relationships in church, home, and society at large shall bear witness to Him and not to ourselves.

Finally, be encouraged: whatever good works that are according to God's will which we do shall be rewarded. We may not be rewarded today; nevertheless, we shall be rewarded in the day of

Christ when we shall appear before His judgment seat (II Corinthians 5:10; I Corinthians 3:14).

Our heavenly Father, how we praise and thank Thee that it is Thy desire to see Thy house built and set in order. We do pray that we may learn from Thy word how Thou dost raise up leadership in the church. Father, we do acknowledge that we are unworthy, that we have no ambition to lead, but if Thou dost call, we pray that we will not shrink back but that by Thy grace we may learn to lead by serving sacrificially. And we pray that Thy church may not be in disorder but that we may know what discipline in our lives is so that we may be able to exercise discipline in love, in priestly spirit and in the power of the Holy Spirit. Oh, how we do pray that there may be sound teaching in Thy church which will produce good works to Thy glory. Oh, we do want to see Thy church built everywhere as lampstands lifting up Christ not only in this land but all over the world as a testimony to Thy goodness and Thy greatness. Oh Father, this is the prayer of our hearts. We do commit one another into Thy hands and to the word of Thy grace. In the name of our Lord Jesus we pray. Amen.

TITLES AVAILABLE
from Christian Fellowship Publishers
By Watchman Nee

ORDER FROM: 11515 Allecingie Parkway Richmond, VA 23235
www.c-f-p.com

TITLES AVAILABLE
from Christian Fellowship Publishers

By Stephen Kaung

Abiding in God
Acts
"But We See Jesus"—*the Life of the Lord Jesus*
Discipled to Christ—*As Seen in the Life of Simon Peter*
God's Purpose for the Family
Government and Ministry in the Local Church
The Gymnasium of Christ
In the Footsteps of Christ
The Key to "Revelation" – Vol. 1
The Key to "Revelation" – Vol. 2
Moses, the Servant of God
New Covenant Living & Ministry
Now We See the Church—*the Life of the Church, the Body of Christ*
Shepherding
The Songs of Degrees—*Meditations on Fifteen Psalms*
The Splendor of His Ways—*Seeing the Lord's End in Job*
Titus

The "God Has Spoken" Series
Seeing Christ in the Old Testament, Part One
Seeing Christ in the Old Testament, Part Two
Seeing Christ in the New Testament

ORDER FROM: 11515 Allecingie Parkway Richmond, VA 23235
www.c-f-p.com